MY WAR BEYOND

VIETNAM

★ ★ ★ ★ ★ ★

IN A WAR WITH NO WINNERS, ROGER HELLE
FOUND SOMETHING HE COULD NEVER LOSE.

AS TOLD TO EZRA COPPIN

Regal Books
A Division of GL Publications
Ventura, California, U.S.A.

Dedication

To the men who fought in Vietnam.

To my beautiful wife Shirley.

To Dave and Gwen Wilkerson for their inspiration
in our lives.

Published by Regal Books
A Division of GL Publications
Ventura, California 93006
Printed in U.S.A.

Scripture quotations in this book are from:
NASB—New American Standard Bible. © The Lockman Foundation
1960, 1972, 1973, 1968, 1971, 1972, 1973, 1975. Used by permission.
KJV—King James Version—Authorized King James Version.

Previously published under the title *Too Proud to Die.*

Library of Congress Cataloging in Publication Data

Helle, Roger.
    My war beyond Vietnam.

    Rev. ed. of: Too proud to die. © 1982.
    1. Helle, Roger. 2. Christian biography—United States.
3. Vietnamese Conflict, 1961-1975—Personal narratives, American.
I. Coppin, Ezra. II. Helle, Roger. Too proud to die. III. Title.
BR1725.H44A37   1985   280′.4′0924   85-30177
ISBN 0-8307-1144-9

2 3 4 5 6 7 8 9 10 / 91 90 89 88

Rights for publishing this book in other languages are contracted
by Gospel Literature International (GLINT) foundation. GLINT
also provides technical help for the adaptation, translation, and
publishing of Bible study resources and books in scores of languages worldwide. For further information, contact GLINT, Post
Office Box 488, Rosemead, California, 91770, U.S.A., or the
publisher.

Contents

Contents

Foreword

In years gone by, a society was only as strong as its warriors. Today, thanks to sociological and technological advances, mankind is capable of turning its hands and minds to pursuits other than killing, at least for short periods of time.

However, man still erupts all too often into the frenzied, nationalistic exercise he calls war. Our warriors are still with us.

Among these modern campaigners, there is always an elite; and in this country, they are the Marines. To be a Marine means you are the best our country has to offer the cause of warfare, and Roger Helle was a Marine.

Not only was Roger one of the few and the proud, but he was one of the best of the best, able to handle anything in any situation, until he came face to face with the angel of death.

Roger is still a warrior. I've been privileged to fight by his side, doing battle with the devil for the souls of the young.

My War Beyond Vietnam is the unforgettable story of a warrior's road to love and happiness, and his enlistment in the army of the King.

Mike Warnke

Introduction

The Vietnam War was probably the most controversial conflict in which the United States was ever involved. Its moral issues will be debated for decades.

Notwithstanding, the men who fought there were heroes in their own right. They struggled in appalling conditions, were frequently frustrated on account of insufficient resources, and often were asked to perform incredible feats.

The true Vietnam hero is epitomized in Roger Helle. Brave to the point of fanaticism, he was all that a U.S. Marine represents. From the wounds of the battlefield, he entered the Valley of Death. By a dying promise to God, he made it back to life. Then in the new battle of life he dedicated himself to the good of the new generation of American youth.

And in this battle, Helle fights a new war beyond Vietnam.

1
The Point Man Falls

The sun shone fitfully between the blackness of heavy clouds. The grass on the open field was still wet from the recent downpour. It was a typical Vietnam morning.

Roger's men were gathered together behind a clump of bushes on the west side of the field. He was briefing them for the sweep he had planned. They were good men, tried and true. They were United States Marines. The fact that they were alive was proof enough of the ability of their squad leader, Sergeant Roger Helle.

"You guys take the south and the rest take the north," Roger said. "I'll run point, but first I want to scout the field for booby traps and mines. Stay covered. I'll be back in a few shorts." With a quick look at his squad to determine whether they understood his instructions, Roger slid out into the open field.

Len, a lance corporal, looked at Roger as he moved away. He turned to the squad with a helpless gesture and said, "The guy's nuts! He was here in 1965. It's now 1970, and his luck still holds. He's one gung-ho marine. If he wasn't so goshdarned lucky, I'd expect him to go this time. He's got to be out of his mind to move out into the open by himself."

"I figure he's a little crazy in the head," said Tom, Len's counterpart in the other half of the squad. "The dumb fool is sitting pretty for promotion, but he'll probably never live to get it."

"For sure," he continued, "he's the gutsiest marine I've ever known. He'd go to hell and back for his men . . . just naturally got to like the guy."

Len and Tom, peering through the bushes in the general direction Roger had taken, saw him from time to time. He was crouched low and moving as though he were on the easiest part of an easy assignment. From time to time, Roger stopped to mark the location of a Viet Cong trap or land mine, making it safe for his men.

The lance corporals turned to the two groups of waiting men. "I guess Roger the Dodger is going to make it again," Len said, "so we better get ready to shove out. He's got more lives than a cat." Then, thoughtfully he added, "It's just as well for us that he has, or we'd all have been dead long ago!"

Soft-spoken John, the squad medical corpsman uttered, "I sure hope he makes it. I'd hate to have to go out there and get him." Someone in the squad laughed uneasily. The tension was mounting as the sweep came nearer to reality. Roger would be back any time.

"Aw, Doc," Len said, "none of those bullets has his name on it. He lives a charmed life."

"Mom and I sure hope you're right," answered John. He was just eighteen years old, doing his first tour of Vietnam. The six-foot, two-inch sergeant was a grizzled veteran at twenty-two years of age.

"Hey, Len," Tom said, "I'll push out and see if I can spot him. Chances are he'll come up to us without any of us seeing him. He's like a thief in the night."

Tom reached out from behind the bushes and looked slit-eyed at the open field. What he saw was to remain in his mind for the rest of his natural life—something he wished he had neither seen nor heard. Roger was two hundred yards away, with his back towards his men. Suddenly a sickening blast threw Roger backward to the ground.

The squad peered from behind the bushes. "My God," one man said, "what happened?"

Looking sick to his stomach, Tom replied, "He got it. A land mine or grenade blew on him. May as well figure to bring the pieces in. Just no way he could have survived."

Len said, "I just don't believe it. He's getting up! We gotta get him out." Amazingly Roger was struggling to get to his feet.

"Wait," said Tom. About forty yards beyond Roger stood a North Vietnamese soldier with his rifle aimed at the wounded man. The squad saw the rifle recoil and heard the familiar snap of the shot once, then twice. Both rounds hit Roger, throwing him to the ground again.

"He got him in the stomach," one of the marine privates said. "Of all the luck! What a way to die. There's just nothing like a clean heart job, or a round that takes off your head."

The squad saw the enemy soldier walk over to where Roger's body lay. They were afraid to move, not knowing what size the enemy group was behind him. They figured the enemy point man got their point man.

As they watched, the North Vietnamese soldier pushed his bayonet downwards. It was the ultimate expression of hatred.

It was too much for Tom. He dropped to one knee, saying as he did, "Let him rot in hell!" He squeezed the round off and the enemy soldier fell. "It won't bring Roger back," Tom said, "but it makes me feel good."

The squad looked in the direction of where Roger's body lay. They loved their brave, stupid, glorious point man, and they realized they would never see him out front again.

Doc said, "I'm going to get him. Give me covering fire. Those swine are not going to mutilate his body. Shoot for their guts if they show. Let them feel it like Roger got it."

2
Out of Obscurity

"Mom, where did Daddy go? He hasn't been here for such a long time."

Roger's mother looked up at her son from the pile of clothes on the ironing board. Her face was expressionless as she answered. "I don't know, sonny. I guess if he wanted us to know where he was, he'd let us know." Pausing a moment, she heaved a deep sigh and continued with the work. "Kids," she breathed. "There isn't any end to the work."

She had brought Roger into the world on October 12, 1947, just after the world was recovering from the horrors of World War II. He was born only ten minutes before his identical twin, Ronald. To add some distinctive note, she gave the name Leigh to Roger and Burton to Ronald. Four years later she gave birth to Theodore, and later Wilma was born. Her husband must have decided married life was too much of a burden, so he left them. She was thinking of those days as she worked.

She had put the twins in an orphanage, for there wasn't anything else to do. She brought them back home when she met their stepfather.

The stepfather had two children of his own when he married Roger's divorced mother and the Helle family began the long years of struggle for survival. In and out of Toledo, Ohio, sometimes in the country and sometimes in the city, they struggled to raise the six children. Roger and Ronald had reached the age when they were asking questions which their mother would just as soon have not answered. There had been little joy in her past life, most of which she just wanted to forget.

She was a tired and sick woman. As the years came and went, she developed neurotic and compulsive habits, which made the lives of the children more difficult.

It was difficult for casual acquaintances to distinguish between Roger and Ronald. They always sat together in school and did everything together. Their clothes were uniformly drab. The one occasion that stood out in their younger years was when they were together in the same confirmation class in the church to which they nominally belonged.

Mother had said, "You must look your best today," and they had been clothed in coarse woven wool suits. The idea of God didn't mean anything to them. Everyone went to confirmation classes and took First Communion, so they did, too.

"You are ready for life now," their mother said. The twins neither knew how nor why.

Roger grew into a tall, skinny kid and did nothing to make his mark, either physically or academically. Ronald applied himself to his books, at least better than his brother. Both made it to 1965 with hopes of graduating at the end of the school year.

Toward the end of the last semester there was a great commotion on their high school campus. A recruitment officer of the United States Marines set up his table in the school and began to persuade the boys of the graduating class to sign up.

Roger pulled Ronald aside one day and said, "Ron, let's join the marines!"

"Are you crazy?" Ronald answered. "They wouldn't want us. We aren't good enough for them."

"I'll bet you a malt they do," Roger replied. "We're both eligible and fit and we're both tall. I bet we could become officers if we wanted to." Roger bellied the words grandiosely and swung an exaggerated salute at his brother. Most of the things they did were initiated by him, but Ronald would usually go along for the ride, while doing equally well later at what had been started.

"Roger," Ronald said, "if I became a marine, I would want to be the best marine there was."

"Yep," Roger answered, "me too! As a matter of fact, we would be the best. What do you say?"

"It's a little scary though," Ronald answered. "That fighting over in Vietnam is getting worse. We might end up there and get killed!"

"The hell we would," Roger replied. "There's no bullet that's got our names on it. I'm going to be something if I do join." He stood tall and hit his chest a resounding blow with his fist. "Sergeant Helle reporting for duty, sir!" he boasted. Then he leaned over to whisper in Ronald's ear. Whatever he said seemed to please his brother. Ronald grinned from ear to ear and excitedly replied, "OK! OK! Let's do it now."

Together, they made their way to the recruiting table and offered their bodies and souls to the United

States Marine Corps, a sacrifice to ambition and patriotism. The officer was delighted to have two tall young men and joshed with them as he signed them in.

"Maybe you'll both end up as generals. At least until the end of the school year you'll be popular on campus." He didn't know that the prospect of admiring girls and envious guys was the lure which Roger had used to reel in his brother!

The last months sped away. Their names were called along with the other six hundred graduating students. High school was a page of history. It had happened just as the man suggested. They were among a few elite graduates who were entering the Marine Corps, and their personal popularity, never previously high, had been enviable in the final months. The girls ooohed and aaahed, and Roger got his first heavy dates.

The last months of school had gone too fast. Roger and his brother had no sooner graduated than very official letters arrived at their home from the Marine Corps. They were to be inducted. They were about to become somebodies.

Roger said, "Hey, Ron, we are going to be important. No more bad food and chores. No more people pushing us around or looking down on us because we are poor. We're even going to get to go to Detroit to be inducted. How 'bout that? We're going to be free at last!"

Traditional Americanism seemed to be born in both boys in that moment. They never knew that most of their assumptions were wrong. They knew, though, that they were going to be the greatest and best United States Marines there ever had been.

A week later, they stood together with other

recruits to be sworn in as marines. Throughout the long bus trip to Detroit they had grown more and more excited. "San Diego, here I come!" Roger shouted, waving good-bye to his mother and stepfather. With a mounting sense of anticipation, the boys believed they had really arrived.

The ceremony was over. It was the last time either was to know the respect due to free men, until 1970 when Roger left the Corps. Noncommissioned officers began to scream and yell at the dazed young men. They were herded and hassled, cursed and abused. The molding of the marine mentality had begun. Later, this hard training would save their lives over and over again, but in that moment it seemed to be one ghastly mistake.

"My God," Roger said, "they treat us like cattle." He was already two inches over six feet tall and his massive fists clenched in protest. He was ready to hit somebody. A cool voice cut into his anger.

"Steady, fella. We all felt the same. It isn't as bad as it sounds. It's just the way marines are. Later you'll think nothing of it." Roger turned to see a grey-haired veteran, his eyes twinkling with humor. Roger immediately felt better.

Sixteen recruits were bundled onto a plane for San Diego. The plane touched down at 1:00 A.M., and a huge, brutal drill instructor was there to continue the mental barrage. During the short ride to the San Diego Marine Corps Recruit Training Depot the DI fired off countless rounds of abuse at the men.

"You're a bunch of scurvy bums," he shouted. "Your hair is filled with lice. I'll take care of that when we arrive. Sharpen yourselves up! What do you think this is? The army? You want to be marines, then look like marines.

"Didn't your mothers teach you how to wash? You smell like dead fish." The exhausted recruits tried desperately to meet the DI's requirements, but by 3:00 A.M., when the men finally hit their bunks, they were unable to follow his commands intelligently. They had been showered, equipped with marine issue clothing, and shorn like sheep, all the while to the strident profanity of the instructors.

Reveille sounded two hours later. Haggard and worn, the new men from high school fell out of bed. They were marched to the chow hall to eat food worse than they had ever tasted at home. They were taken to the garbage cans and were lined up beside them. The DI said, "Some day you'll eat worse than what's there!"

Roger was suddenly violently sick. As in everything, Ronald joined him. Vomiting over themselves as they stood at attention, their humiliation was complete.

Back in the bunkroom, Roger looked at Ronald and said, "Damn it! They got the better of me once. It will never happen again. Ronald, from today, we beat the Marine Corps. We must be meaner, tougher, and harder than any instructor. Got it?" Ronald nodded his head slowly. They were both thinking of the high and lofty ideals which they had held following the day of their enlistment.

Ronald agreed, "Roger, let's be good marines. They can't beat us unless we let them. Let's be among the best in this intake."

Roger's lips broke in a twisted smile as he replied, "I am the best. Only three men will leave here as privates first class. I plan to be one of them. Remember, we thought we could be officers? I plan to be an officer and a gung-ho marine. It may be a long pull, Ron, but I'll make it. It is the only chance I'll ever have to be something different. I plan to use it."

Roger and Ronald were seventeen and one-half years of age. They held together in boot camp. The rougher the training, the more they concentrated on beating the obstacles. In many personal exchanges they confirmed to one another the intention of completing basic training with promotion to private first class. They held each other up in this determination.

Finally it was over. Private First Class Roger Helle was sent to the infantry. Private First Class Ronald Helle was routed into the artillery. Their goals were achieved, but the pathways divided.

Roger sat one night in his Camp Pendleton barracks making a decision which would affect his life forever. He muttered to himself, "I joined the marines to fight. I can't just sit here. I'm a 'grunt' with better chances than most. I'm going to volunteer for Vietnam."

Having made the decision to offer to go to Vietnam, it was natural for him to share it with Ronald, who also was determined to be a hero. Both had made a personal commitment to succeed in boot camp, and both had fulfilled the commitment. Both made renewed commitments never to fail, to be the best, to live and, if necessary, to die in the best traditions of the Marine Corps. Ronald would go to Vietnam also.

Roger told his platoon instructor about his wish to go to Vietnam. The instructor, wearing combat ribbons, looked shocked. Peering intently at Roger, he said, "Are you sure that's what you want to do? It isn't funny over there. It's no picnic."

"Sergeant," Roger repeated, "I want to go to Vietnam. I am a combat marine."

"Yeah, yeah. I know," the instructor replied. "I felt the same, but a tour in Vietnam changed my thinking. Marine, I'll forget what you said if you like. What are you trying to be? A hero yet?"

The sergeant never forgot the words of his PFC. "Yes, sir. I intend to be a hero. I plan to be the best marine in the Corps."

There was scorn and pity on the sergeant's face, but also a grudging admiration. Roger was about to turn eighteen years of age, and the veteran marine thought ruefully of his own younger years. Having fought through Korea, he was a career marine.

"OK! If that's what you want, that's what you'll get. Don't say I never told you," the sergeant concluded.

Two days later Roger's orders were cut. It was too late to change his mind. He made his way to Toledo for leave. Ronald had finished basic training a week before Roger and was already home. Part of the time they spent together. Apart from rare meetings, it was to be the last time they would spend together for years. They went through staging and on to Vietnam by separate routes.

3
Into the Valley of Death

"Marine, if you are as goofy in Vietnam as you are here, you'll be dead inside a month." The NCO was brutal and frank. The special training unit for the Vietnam War was rougher than anything Roger had ever known. Roger must have appeared as a lanky, kooky idiot, caught up in some glamorous idea about war. He was all fingers and thumbs. It seemed impossible for him to slide in the grass noiselessly, or to steal through the brush without making a sound. The instructors seemed to be trying to tear him into pieces and flush the shreds down the sewer.

Despite the discouragements, Roger impressed the staging unit with his recklessness. The barracks talked for weeks about the time when he threw himself into a bunker at Camp Pendleton and landed squarely on top of the largest rattlesnake ever killed on the base. Roger smashed it to pieces with his rifle. Later he lost another weapon in a flash flood.

His training sergeant reported to the operation officer. "He is crazy! He makes more mistakes than I have ever seen, but shows more sheer initiative than I can describe. The guy has guts and leadership capability."

The next report on Roger dutifully contained all that the NCO had reported, and his file began to take its form. "Crazy, but a natural fighter. Knows no fear. When he has been into battle and blooded will be leadership quality. It is recommended that his development be observed carefully with a view to future responsibilities."

Finally, the crash program for Vietnam was over. Another contingent of men were entering the valley of the shadow of death. Few of the men expected to return. Vietnam was a remorseless and relentless enemy. Men said good-bye to their families with the quiet expectation that good-bye meant good-bye forever. Roger sent a Western Union message to his mother and prepared to leave.

The day Roger said farewell to Camp Pendleton, he expected his next stop to be Vietnam, but the plane took him to the Philippines. He was part of a select raiding group, the first of its kind since the Korean War. He was there for battalion training in survival. The official designation was "Survival Problem."

The briefing was concise and direct. The lieutenant in charge of the fifteen day operation in the jungle wasted no words. "This is the rice and raisins operation. You will have a sock filled with rice and another filled with raisins. You will live on this for fifteen days. If you fail to make it, you will be dead. If you manage to survive, you will be ready for Vietnam."

Roger turned to a friend and said, "We can always eat worms if we have to. An old friend of my family told me that a man can survive on a diet of worms and leaves. I plan on making it to Vietnam, and if I have to eat worms, I'll eat worms."

His friend replied, "Helle, you are crazier than a bandicoot. Would you eat snakes, too?"

Roger answered, "Rattlesnake is good food. I suppose that most other snakes are edible, too. I'll eat snake if I have to, but one thing is for sure, I am coming in alive and well."

Fifteen days passed and Roger walked into the base camp as fit as the day he left, ready for Vietnam. His officers reported in his record, "This marine has survival capacity and will do well in Vietnam after initial exposure to action."

The Assault Battalion was ready. It was expected to continue the reputation of its predecessor in Korea. The officer in command laid it on the line. He could do so because he had been part of the previous battalion in Korea.

"Don't get the idea this is easy," he bellowed. "We're chosen to do a special job. Any or every part of military action, we are capable of assuming. We can land by air or by sea. We can attack in force, or by select, search-and-destroy teams. We are the living dead. For us, there is little future except the honor of the Corps and the personal satisfaction of having done our duty. Our next stop is Vietnam. You have been trained for this and you are ready. Within a short time you will have killed your first man. If you are squeamish, you are in the wrong fighting force. If you can't kill a man with your bare hands, gouge out the eyes of the enemy in a personal encounter, or shoot a man in cold blood, you do not belong in this unit.

"I will consider the request of any man who is incapable of fulfilling these things. I would sooner transfer you now than prejudice the safety of your fellow marines.

"This battalion is ready. We will distinguish ourselves in battle. You are marines and you have been trained to do anything which must be done to liquidate the enemy. We leave at dawn. I wish you luck. Some of you will die. Die well! Some of you will be wounded. Bear your misfortune with courage. Remember, a marine never whimpers, whines, or complains. We are marines because we chose to be marines."

Roger went quietly to his bunk. He was not afraid, nor did the severity of the commanding officer's bluntness spook him. "I am the marine he described, and I plan to use the opportunities to prove to myself and to my family that I am somebody of whom they may be proud." As he thought these things, a great confidence filled him. "I will be a hero, because I am too proud to be anything else," he reflected.

The battalion was based on an assault carrier off the coast of Vietnam. From it the men exercised every military maneuver for which they had been trained. In rubber rafts and from helicopters they raided the coast. It was the monsoon season. Roger had only just turned eighteen, and yet he enjoyed the activities for which he had been trained.

Up and down the coast they raided villages. There was little action. An occasional sniper's bullet sang by, but little else. In the first month there were no casualties.

Roger chafed. At the beginning of November 1965, reports began to filter through of a hardcore Viet Cong troop activity in the area north of Danang. These troops had been trained by the North Vietnam regulars and were believed of regiment strength. The marines began to plan Operation Harvest Moon. The entire SLF Ops (Special Landing Force Operations) were to be used as a blocking force, four attack companies and the support company. It was the first major operation for Roger. He was in Foxtrot Company, Second Battalion, First Marines.

The company was taken in by helicopter and was set down in a rice paddy immediately in front of an enemy regimental command post. It was the baptism of fire of which his instructors had spoken. The company was pinned under heavy mortar, artillery, and small arms fire. Roger thrilled to his first action. The sight of dead Viet Cong soldiers did not sicken him. He was never nauseated at the sight of death. Harvest Moon was the type of action in which the marines could not register "kills." The sweeping which developed in the breakthrough left hundreds dead, but no one knew who killed them. Roger wanted to kill.

During the action, Danny, a close friend, was killed. He and Roger had trained together, left together, and passed through the Survival Course together. They had been inseparable.

One night after the main sweep was finished, Roger's friend was out on patrol when he was hit three times in the chest by small arms fire. The shock stunned Roger. "By God," he vowed, "I will kill every gook I can." A deep hatred of the enemy began to consume Roger. To him, the only good enemy was a dead enemy. An implacable bitterness rose in him.

"Why did it have to be him?" he asked. His friend was a quiet, likable guy. Roger met Danny's fiancee before he left the U.S. The death seemed useless and unfair. He knew no other way to cope with the problem but to kill, kill, kill. This he promised himself he would do.

One morning, the company commander sent for Roger. He had heard reports of the great bitterness in him and the insatiable desire to kill the enemy.

"Helle," the officer said, "I have my eye on you. You are a damned good marine, the kind that has made the Corps famous. Control your passion. What you do, do with cold, incisive calculation. You have the makings of a leader, but if you do not control your passion, you will end up dead and perhaps lead many others into death with you. Let your hatred of the enemy cool until it is obsessive but not compulsive."

Roger left the interview with thoughtfulness. "To do what I have to do," he pondered, "I must be more calculating." From that day, Roger became a killing machine. He disciplined himself to think how many ways he could kill with a rifle, a grenade, a bayonet, or with his bare hands. He conditioned his mind to be prepared for the real action when it came. Instinctively, he knew the killing had just begun for him. He planned to be ready for it when it did come.

Pete, a close friend, staggered into the base one day from off patrol, with deep puncture wounds in his left foot and right leg made by punji sticks, the sharpened bamboo sticks the enemy would conceal in the grass beside the trails. The enemy would sometimes fire a shot and the men would often stab themselves on the sticks, jumping for cover. The wounded man, already poisoned by the water buffalo manure with which the punji sticks had been coated was barely able to relate what had happened.

Roger cursed. "Pete," he answered, "by all that is sacred, I'll kill a dozen men for what has happened to you." He strode off into the dark, consumed with hatred so intense that the men with him began to fear him.

"He's crazy," they said, "plain loco. It's going to get him killed one day."

A close friend, Manuel, a Latin, added, "There's nothing going to happen to him. He walks without fear." Then in a near whisper he said, *"Sangre de Cristo, ayude mi amigo"* (Blood of Christ, help my friend).

Roger's great height and physical build made him respected by all his friends. One of his closest friends, laughing but serious, commented, "When we get close to the enemy, I hope to have him with me." While the conversation flitted around him, Roger himself grew more and more temperamental and quiet. He seemed to have no time for humor. He was in Vietnam to kill, and if possible, to be a hero while doing it.

4
Operation New York

Back on the aircraft carrier, Roger made mental note of the empty bunks. Operation Harvest Moon had decimated the men with whom he had fought. As he looked up and down the sleeping quarters, the faces of one and another of the missing men flitted across the screen of his mind. They would not be back. Death was so sudden that some had never felt it, and they were the more fortunate, Roger thought. The wounded were in hospitals ashore, and some would live so maimed as to wish they had died. Scores had contracted the curse of the rice paddies, commonly called immersion foot. Men, otherwise healthy, suffered terribly as their feet literally rotted in their boots.

Roger grew grim as he contemplated the empty beds. The great bitterness which consumed him when his close friend Danny had taken three rounds in the chest closed in on him again. He buried his face in his pillow to muffle the screaming curses which rose from his throat. Finally, spent in his anger, he rose off his bed and spoke, to nobody in particular and everyone in general. "By God, they'll pay for it! From this day I'll kill every gook I can lay a gunsight on." Expelling a great gust of air from his mouth, he clenched his fists and shook them above his head. His jaws snapped shut like a trap and his giant frame quivered in frustration.

"Hey, amigo! Cool it," said Manuel. "You can't bring these guys back. It is just one of those things. Today them. Tomorrow it might be us."

"The hell it will," Roger exploded. "They'll never get me. But if they do, I'll take a lot of them out first."

"Yep, I figure you will, amigo," Manuel answered.

Forty percent of the bunks were empty. There was no way to know how many were dead, how many wounded, or how many were missing in action. The one glaring fact remained: the men were not aboard the carrier.

Roger gritted his teeth, still simmering. "I'm going topside to get some air," he said to Manuel. "Maybe I'll get control of my mind by the time I come back."

From the deck, Roger looked off into the haze. Deep down on the horizon was land. "I'll be back," he muttered as he stared at the thin line representing Vietnam. Violent again, he gritted out, "You can bet your dirty lives I'll be back!"

He hadn't heard his company lieutenant approach from behind and was startled to hear himself being addressed by a firm but quiet voice.

"Marine, listen to me," the lieutenant said. It came with the force of an order and Roger's reflexes snapped him to attention.

"Sir?" he queried.

"At ease, marine. Keep that for the parade ground." The officer looked quizzically at Roger and asked informally, "What's bugging you, Helle?"

It was all Roger needed. He let the pent-up anger boil over. The officer listened and nodded his head understandingly.

Then, as though the moment of understanding had never occurred, he shouted, "Marine, attention!" Roger stiffened once more. The lieutenant looked scathingly at Roger and said, "So you're the great marine? I've watched you, Helle. You're good. Damned good, but at the same time, you're no damned good! A well-trained marine has himself in control all the time. Your violence will get you killed. You've been trained as well as any man. Trained to kill and to see men die. Trained to grit your teeth and take it. YOU ARE A MARINE!" The officer was screaming profanity at Roger.

Suddenly the officer was quiet. The soft, warm breeze seemed to calm him. He looked at Roger and spoke again, quietly. "I need you Helle. You're no good dead. Kill all you can. Hate until it hurts, but do not let your emotions push you under. You'll be promoted soon, and I need you cold, calculating, and calm. At ease!" He slapped Roger on the shoulder and strode away.

When he disappeared, Roger whistled under his breath. "Wow, that's one heck of a marine," he thought. Roger was calm at last. He knew the officer was right. His own survival and ability to kill Viet Cong depended upon being alive. He figured for the second time in his career, "I better cool it," and he began the cold hatred mind-set again. The conditioning, which would prepare him for the men he planned to liquidate, began with quiet intensity.

Two days later, Roger's lieutenant stopped him and

said, "I want to talk with you, Helle." He led the way to a shaded spot on the deck and motioned Roger to sit down. "Get comfortable," he said. Roger wondered what he had done.

"Helle, I am off record. OK?" the officer said. Roger gave a shrug of agreement and settled back a little more securely. He just knew he was in some kind of trouble. The lieutenant began, "I think you are leadership material, Helle. I am grooming you from today. I want your cooperation.

"We are going into action soon. We have an airstrip to get organized at Phu Bai, just north of Danang. The Corps is moving northwards towards the Ho Chi Minh Trail. After the airstrip is completed, there is a heavy engagement planned.

"I wanted to alert you, because it is important for you to have yourself under control," he added. "By the way, how are your nerves?"

"I'm fine, lieutenant. I have been getting myself ready for the last couple days. I believe I can handle anything now. I was so damned mad when we came back on board—those empty bunks just blew my mind. It was probably what I needed to get me accustomed to what's ahead."

"I really do understand, Helle," the officer replied. "It seems only yesterday since I went through all the same feelings, but it's really been years. Korea wasn't pretty, either. One of our officers back there did much the same to me as I did to you the other day. It worked for me, too!"

The airstrip at Phu Bai was soon completed and its perimeters established. The war was being stepped up. The Marine Corps was becoming more deeply involved. From Phu Bai, Roger went out, night after night, with small patrols, securing the perimeters. Occasionally, the patrol ran into minor guerrilla action, but not enough to give trouble.

It was February 1966. The fun and games were over. Operation New York was launched. It was about an hour after midnight when the call went out to prepare. The marines at Phu Bai were fully combat ready in a very short time.

"Men," the commanding officer said, "we are being sent to relieve a unit of the Vietnamese army. A hardcore Viet Cong battalion has mauled it very badly. Things are rough out there. This will be a heavy engagement. Remember your training and do your best as marines. Good luck!"

Two companies went out by helicopter. It was one of the first night operations of the war. One marine company was landed as a blocking force and the other deployed as a sweeping unit. The men were tense as they landed. Flares lit the area and the men dug in. There was a lot of confusion.

It seemed forever until dawn. As the day broke, the men were quickly organized into their positions. Roger was sweeping, a back-and-forth movement to make sure an area was clear of enemy troops. The company was trying to cut off the retreat of the Viet Cong. It was the first really close action for Roger. His mind was clear and his nerves were steady.

The sweep lasted all morning. At noon, as the heat blazed down, Roger was right out in front of the first wave. The marines ran into a maze of punji sticks as they approached a tree line. It was a sure indication of trouble.

Fifty yards from the tree line, all hell seemed to break loose. The marines were as near to the tree line as they could be without actually seeing into the trees. The entire Viet Cong battalion had dug in under the cover of the forest. Everything came apart. The marines were still in the open when small arms fire, machine gun and mortar fire, and grenades began to pour out.

Roger hit the dirt. "Dear God," he breathed and hugged the earth. He was immediately in front of a .50mm machine gun position, from which a deadly spray was coming all along the front.

Roger heard the terrible agony of the dying. Two men on his left were hit immediately. A lance corporal was hit in the chest by full fire from the .50mm machine gun. Roger turned in time to hear the man shriek and see him blown down. The body fell near enough for Roger to see the ugly wounds. The body twitched and then lay still.

"Keep low," Roger bellowed at the men near him. A PFC didn't listen and was mowed down at the legs as if a scythe had cut across his pathway. Roger's staff sergeant looked up. Roger yelled, "Get down, sergeant!" It was too late. The man's head seemed to disintegrate. Another man, hit in the jugular vein, was dead within a minute or two.

The marines were dead if they stayed there and dead if they moved. The lieutenant chose the slightly better option. "Let's go," he cried and was out and running with the men. The tree line seemed a mile away. Men fell to Roger's left and right. Screams of agony merged into the chaos of the chatter of machine guns and mortars.

A mortar exploded in front of Roger, staggering him and knocking him down. He lay quiet. Then sheer horror grabbed at his insides. He was lying across a leg. Somebody's leg! Then he was up and running again. He thought, "It was only a leg!"

Again he fell. Where he hit the ground, he was lying beside the torso of a Viet Cong soldier. Roger felt good. He wondered if the leg had been a part of the torso, and laughing and screaming, he ran on.

Air strikes and artillery brought relief. Foxtrot Company was halved. Over 50 percent of the marines were dead or dying, but the remainder pressed on. The Viet Cong soldiers were caught in a trap from which they could not escape. They were eliminated and some prisoners were taken. Some were loaded on a helicopter and taken back for interrogation. It was cruel, brutal, and bloody war.

Back in Phu Bai, Roger was warmed to have the lieutenant tell him, "Good work, Helle! You were cool and in control. You'll be OK now. Keep it up!"

5
Kill Them Quickly

Life in Phu Bai was anything but pleasant. Every man knew that just around the corner was another action. Roger couldn't get the word soon enough. His killing instinct was coming into focus.

"Helle," he heard a voice calling. He turned to see from what direction the call came. He saw his lieutenant some hundred yards away, making his way towards Roger, and waited.

Finally the lieutenant caught up to Roger and asked him to spend a few minutes with him. Roger consented, although not with much enthusiasm. Conferences of this kind often spelled some kind of special assignment. His thinking was dead right.

"I told you, Helle, that you were one damned good marine and that I was watching you for the development of leadership roles. I have such an opportunity to offer you. It will be satisfying, but it's not without danger.

"We are commencing a new program in which an NCO will accompany a chosen group of marines and live in the villages with them. The groups will both protect and train the villagers against guerrilla activities. It is a kind of neutralization and pacification program. We'll be calling for volunteers in a day or so. The job carries some risk, but will give you a chance of promotion. Do you think you would be interested? I think you will do very well on night patrols and supervision of the village people. Think it over and let me know when the call goes out. OK?"

Roger said little. He wanted time to think. If he went out into the villages, he would have command of his own, even if only a little. If he declined the opportunity, he would be in some major action within a short time and go in as one of the infantry grunts. "I guess I am a grunt," he thought, "but I would like to have some responsibility other than staying alive." He decided to accept the challenge of the new job.

In March of 1966 the call came for volunteers. There wasn't any great enthusiasm among the marines, but Roger was there with his boots on.

"Hey, man!" he confided to his officer. "I'm going out there for better or for worse. It couldn't be worse than hanging around here and certainly no worse than another nasty, major sweep."

"I'm happy you have decided to go, Helle. It will give you the break you need. You've got it together. Just keep your cool and let the old nerves stay calm. I'll be rooting for you!"

Out in the villages, Roger found his special niche. He soon found that the militia of the South was divided into two groups. The PFs, or Popular Forces, were local militia from the actual village structures. The RFs, or Regular Forces, were better trained and on a regional basis. Both groups were dedicated and loyal to the cause of anti-Communism.

Night after night, Roger volunteered for patrol. The assignments were desperately dangerous, but Roger revelled in the spicy and challenging work.

The sergeant-in-charge asked him one day, "Why do you always want patrol? Even more importantly, why do you keep volunteering for point duty? Are you trying to get killed, or just hoping for a nice comfortable wound that will get you home?"

The marine sergeant had to back off from the anger of the man whom he was questioning. There was blazing fury in Roger's eyes as he clenched his fists and spat through his teeth. "Sergeant, don't ever ask me that again! I'll answer the question one time. Get it straight and you won't have to ask me again. OK?"

"Aw, come on, Helle," the sergeant drawled. "What's eatin' on you?"

"It's like this sergeant. I am a marine. I am the best there is. I'm not bragging; it just happens to be the truth. I am here for one purpose—to kill the most gooks I can kill. One day during Operation Harvest Moon, my best buddy got it. Then another close buddy got impaled with punji sticks. When I saw him, he was far gone. I swore I would avenge their deaths. I don't plan to be any hero, but I do plan to do what I was trained to do. If I get to be a hero at the same time, it will make me happy. I'll do my best to stay alive, but if it is all the same to you, I'll run point on patrol."

Roger was still only eighteen years of age, but the sergeant looked at him with a new respect and made a mental note about the leadership ability of his PFC.

"Gung-ho," he judged. "One hell of a man to meet on a dark night if you were a Viet Cong guerrilla. I wouldn't want to get him riled up with me." Roger was showing the physical development of a twenty-five-year-old man and the courage of a veteran. He still had not consciously killed his first man, but kept looking for the chance to be blooded in that special way. He didn't have long to wait.

Roger volunteered for nighttime patrols. They were more dangerous and a greater challenge to his sixth sense. The lives of the men with him depended on him, and this challenged the best in him.

Initially, Roger was a lousy point. He made too much noise and goofed where more experienced men would not have failed. On one occasion he led the patrol out and suddenly disappeared from sight.

"My God," one of the men said, "where did that b——— go? Now we see him; now we don't." Roger had walked over a sheer drop of twenty-five feet. He smashed his third rifle. Badly shaken and with several cracked ribs, Roger was recovered by his patrol, which teased him unmercifully.

"Hey, Roger!" one man razzed. "What if you had fallen into a bed of poisonous snakes or spiders. They don't give Purple Hearts for falling over cliffs. Besides, we might all have come after you!"

Roger was angry at himself and humiliated at the danger into which he had brought his patrol. He remembered he had sworn to be the best. He bit his lip and answered, "Fella, I just wanted a new rifle." The joking lasted a week and then was forgotten, for Roger was becoming the best point man on the lines. He was developing uncanny instinct. The men beat a pathway to the sergeant to try to pull his patrol as their nightly assignment.

At dusk one night, Roger led his patrol by an alternate route to the ambush site he had predetermined during the day. Running point as usual, he rounded a corner and saw a man crouched against a hedgerow of bushes which surrounded a mud hut. The bushes were about waist high.

The villager was stooped down beside the bushes at the entrance to the yard of the hut. He was wearing a utility-type shirt, typical of the surplus military gear which was always available, either by trade or from the bodies of dead men. The man was looking in the opposite direction and peering down the trail.

Roger came up behind him and tapped him on the shoulder with his rifle, giving him a cordial smile, thinking him to be a friendly villager. "Give me your ID card," Roger demanded. The man smiled back and shook his head, replying in Vietnamese, "Not understand, not understand!" As the dialogue progressed, Roger heard voices approaching to his left. He looked in that direction and saw two Viet Cong guerrillas emerging, in uniform. Their rifles were shoulder slung. Roger darted a glance back at the man by the bushes and was startled to see him pulling out a Chicom (Chinese Communist) grenade. The sight of the grenade made him realize he was confronted with a crisis situation. The man was slowly backing away as he withdrew the potato-masher type grenade.

Faster than greased lightning Roger moved. For this hour he had been trained, brainwashed, and prepared. With his right hand he reached for the man's shirt. He threw him to the ground at his feet. Faster than the eye could follow, Roger whipped the muzzle of his 7.62mm M.14 rifle on the man's chest and pulled the trigger. Without breaking the rhythm of his movement, with every instinct alert, he dropped to his knee, facing the two Viet Cong guerrillas. They were desperately trying to unshoulder their rifles. They never made it in time.

Roger's rifle was spraying death even as his knee hit the ground. The men were only about twenty feet away, and they literally disintegrated as the huge bullets of the M.14 smashed into them. About three of the twenty rounds in the magazine had ripped into the chest of the first man. The other soldier was cut across the chest and stomach with what was left. The magazine was empty.

The patrol leader rushed up from his position further back, expecting to find Roger dead. He burst out, "Helle, are you still alive?" Roger laughed the laugh of the victor. In five seconds he had killed three men. His training had stood him in good stead and his reflexes had proven out perfectly. He stood proudly before his leader. "Sergeant, I don't plan on being anything else. I'm here to kill, not be killed!"

The whole episode had happened so quickly there had been no time for thought. Instinct, the killer instinct of a highly trained machine, had won out over the threat of death. Roger was elated. He was now a fully-blooded killer of gooks. In a few seconds he developed a new level of maturity. Even before the patrol leader arrived, Roger had turned the bodies over with his foot. The men were very dead. The enemy had been carrying AK 47 assault rifles, the most modern the Viet Cong possessed. None had been seen in the area before, but their weapons had not prevailed against one crazy marine who had sworn to avenge his friends, to be a perfect, logical killing machine and become a hero. He was on his way, at eighteen and one-half years of age. He could smell the promotions and decorations. He felt no remorse.

Roger thought of Danny and was very pleased with himself.

6
War Is Hell

It finally happened. Roger was made lance corporal, and the close observations of his superiors began to pay off.

"Helle," the lieutenant said, "I want you to take a squad of men and patrol this area." He pointed on the map to a region of dense forest. Roger knew it was shot through with trails and held strong possibility of ambush.

"Yes, sir," Roger complied. His heart was light, full of excitement and anticipation as he mustered his men. He was getting the first real opportunity to claw his way up the success ladder. He didn't plan on losing the chance which was offered.

"Fellas," he said to the patrol, "this is a dangerous area. I'll take point. Keep your eyes skinned, move quietly, and don't get your heads blown off."

Thirty minutes later, eleven men were dead. The Viet Cong were so hidden as to delude Roger, even though by this time his reputation on point was quite established. He got two men out alive. It was a bitter day in his life. His two men who survived were sent back to the States. Their eardrums had been shattered in the roar of grenades.

Roger swore vengeance again. The longer he served the more he determined to kill before he was killed. The struggle wasn't fierce enough for him, and he sought more active duty. He was now a finely honed killing machine. He had seen enough to complete the resolutions he had made earlier. While he waited on the results of his application for a more active area, he had time to think about the horror of war. War was hell!

Some time previously, Roger had been part of a patrol which found a village chief massacred, along with his family.

The patrol had cautiously approached the village. It was strangely quiet. The teeth of the marines were on edge. The area smelled like trouble.

"I don't like this," the sergeant said. "Let's just wait out here and look the place over for a while."

Nothing happened. The eerie stillness continued. Finally the sergeant said, "Go on, Helle. Find out what's with this place. Hit the deck if anything starts. We'll be right behind you. Be careful! There is something weird about this place. There's not even a dog around."

Roger worked his way to the village. He felt his skin erupt in prickles and a shiver went down his spine. Closer and closer he crawled. Then he understood.

Roger was around a slight bend and out of sight of the patrol when he saw the reason for the unusual, deathlike feeling. He stared unbelievingly. His mouth framed the expletive, but the words never came out. Pure blind rage cut them off. He was riveted into absolute immobility as he looked across the space between where he lay and where the village proper began.

"Oh, those b————-!" He cursed and rose quickly to his feet. He glanced ahead and to each side. Everything was ghostly and still. Without reporting, Roger ran the intervening distance to the village. He was sprinting, crouched low, but without thought of possible danger.

Outside the village gate, a pole had been secured to the fence. On the top of the pole was the severed head of the village chief. Roger had known him well, as a wise, gentle man who was loved by his people.

The head leered grotesquely at Roger. For the first time in Vietnam, he was sick in his stomach. Rage and nausea tore at him simultaneously. The emotions and feelings were held in check by their offsetting value. At the foot of the pole lay a naked body. It was that of the chief.

The Viet Cong guerrillas who had killed the chief had first stripped and tortured him. "I'll bet he was alive when they did it," Roger thought. The enemy had hacked off the man's genitals and stuffed them into his mouth. There were no other wounds on the head, so Roger figured that, following the mutilation, the enemy had beheaded the chief.

Roger heard a rustle beside a hut. Instantly ready to fire, he paused. A young boy appeared, his face contorted with fear. Roger beckoned him and the boy approached slowly. His voice had frozen in his throat. He looked at Roger a moment and beckoned him to follow. Twenty-five yards inside the village lay the naked body of a pregnant woman. Her distended belly had been slashed open to bare the child in her womb. A terrible smell came from the corpse.

"What happened, boy?" he asked.

Very slowly, the boy explained the raid. The guerrillas had come unexpectedly. The villagers fled to the forest. The raiders let them go, but kept the chief and his family. The chief's little daughter, about nine years of age, was raped by many men as the anguished father and mother were forced to watch. When she was cast aside, village women had picked her up and fled to the sanctuary of the forest.

It was the wife and mother next. She was stripped and pinned to the ground and slashed open. The woman had screamed in agony until her mouth was effectively silenced by a dirty rag.

Three men lined up beside the woman. She was conscious and seemed to know what was being done to her. One by one the men urinated into the abdominal cavity. The urine spilled onto the ground.

As the boy described the scene, he began to shake violently. The rehearsal was too much for him. Roger put his arm around the boy and comforted him.

"What then?" Roger asked.

"She just die," the boy replied. Roger realized the woman had died in agony beyond description. It was an Asian death, reserved for those who were meant to suffer complete agony before death. Roger looked down. The wound was filled with flies, and maggots were already crawling throughout it.

"What then?" Roger asked again.

"He die like you see," came the boy's answer. Roger knew there was nothing he could do. He walked back to the patrol and told them what he had found. The marines clenched their fists, cursed, and promised themselves to repay another debt. They called the patrol off and went back to make report.

Yes, war was hell. The more he thought about it, the more Roger realized it. The more he realized it, the more he wanted to kill.

Then came a day of death.

Roger's patrol was out again. The squad made contact with a Viet Cong guerrilla unit. The enemy broke for cover, and the marines poured small arms fire towards them. One man was killed.

The sergeant turned the body over with his foot. "Well, I'll be damned," he said. "Who'd have thought it. He was such a nice guy!"

The patrol clustered around. They were looking down into the face of their barber, now dead. The men whistled with shock.

Someone remarked, "He cut my hair yesterday." Another laughed and said, "Yep, his razor was on my neck yesterday."

It really wasn't funny, but the men laughed anyway. It was Vietnam. The man who walked by men as a friend might at the same time be a venomous enemy and be plotting sudden death. Few knew who was the enemy. The enemy was a philosophy, something alien and almost intangible. The enemy was, nevertheless, real and always there.

Roger remembered how, on that occasion, he had laughed with the rest. It was mirthless. "Damn, he was supposed to cut my hair tomorrow. What's a good marine going to do for a barber now?"

The guys had roared. One wit remarked, "Good barbers are hard to get. Let's nip over to L.A. for a cut." Roger felt then the deeply engrained cynicism in that quip. The men knew they were there to die, but most wanted to go out well, not killed by someone who had fronted as a friend.

Then there was the dysentery. Roger remembered that also. The war went on, dysentery or not. Roger had been standing at the gate of the village. It was just coming nightfall, and his patrol was ready to move out again. Roger was loading his rifle. He moved and his bowels literally gushed out, down his legs and into his boots. The smell was really bad and the men moved away.

Roger turned to the corporal and called out, "Corporal!" but the NCO merely shrugged and replied, "Go!" Roger was point that night. As he led out, the wind blew in his face and carried the stench back to the patrol. The ribald wit flew as the men ridiculed him.

The patrol that night was expected to intercept a tax raid by the Viet Cong. The marines set up on a hillside opposite the village where the taxing was to happen. The corporal came that night and ordered, "Helle, take the rear security. You'll be out of range!"

The raid was to be about midnight. Roger was over the crest of the hill. At 1:00 A.M., when nothing had yet occurred, Roger made his way back towards where the patrol had been. There were no marines there. They had left and pulled out, forgetting their smelly friend.

Roger decided to stay put. It was suicide to do otherwise, he decided. He lay down in his own filth to sleep. His sleep was rudely interrupted. The raid was on, an hour later than expected.

Roger counted ten men. They entered the huts and extracted money and food from the villagers. Roger was within action distance. It was his time for the Congressional Medal of Honor, but there would be nobody to attest his valor.

Roger had five magazines and three grenades. He mulled over the situation and chuckled whimsically as he thought, "What would John Wayne have done?" But then, John Wayne never had recorded dysentery!

He estimated that by throwing the grenades first and then opening up with his rifle he could take out about six of the enemy, but he knew he could not get them all.

As he thought reflectively back on that night, he recalled his words, spoken to the ink of the night. "What's the use of being a hero if nobody is going to know about it?" He figured to let the enemy go. Roger simply had to sit and watch the raid develop and finish. He made his way back near dawn, grateful that he had not been the first marine to be killed while his bowels moved.

Beyond all argument, war was hell!

7
They Called Him Lucky

Back in Phu Bai, a legend was beginning to grow. Roger's Combined Action unit had its headquarters there, and the village unit was under direct radio control from its lieutenant at that base. It was common news around Phu Bai that there was a marine NCO up front who was born under some lucky star. Roger's incredible sixth sense as point man and his inexplicable ability to stay alive was common talk. The lieutenant told the captain, and the captain told the colonel. It was mess hall discussion.

"The guy's the best marine we've got in the area," his lieutenant said. "We ought to make him some rank. He's a natural leader."

A fellow officer remarked, "Let's give him a little more time and take a serious look at him. God knows we need good men. I saw some of the reports on him. It seems everyone has felt he was potential leadership material. Let's leave him another month or so. If his luck holds, I'd be in favor of promoting him." So it was decided.

Roger became known along the marine front as

Lucky. As men were killed or wounded in the village unit, replacements asked to be a part of the outfit where Lucky ran point.

Up in the village, the unit was seething. An inviolable law was being broken. The men were angry, even mutinous. Phu Bai had commanded them to make a night patrol on the same trail two nights in a row.

The unit sergeant was hopping mad. "They must be trying to get our heads blown off. It's a good thing I am a marine, for nobody else would obey the ——— order!"

Out on point, Roger was meticulously careful. He knew that a patrol which went over its own steps while they were warm would most probably end up cold for a long time. As he led out, he turned to the men and grinned. When he spoke, it was a comfort to them. "I'm not called Lucky for nothing! I'll get you through. Trust me."

The patrol seemed to last forever. The men were nervous. Even the sergeant was uneasy. Only a dozen years as a career marine kept his mind on the job. Roger brought them through, and as they clustered around the chow table back at the village, one of the guys laughed and said, "Roger, what'll happen to us when you get yours?"

There was a moment of acute tension. Comments of that nature were definitely out. They were considered in poor taste and very unlucky. The men fidgeted uneasily and wondered how Roger would react. His answer was slow in coming, but when it came, it eased the tension.

"You stupid idiot, I ought to stuff your tongue down your throat for saying such a dumb thing," Roger replied. "By the time you've been here as long as I have, you'll know better than to push your ——— luck by shooting your lip about something like that! But, . . ." and Roger waited one expressive moment, "because I am lucky, stick around. I'm going nowhere you wouldn't want to go!"

Roger strode over to the offending marine and slapped him hard on the shoulder in a friendly way. Then he said, "Stick with Lucky, kid! As long as I'm on point, you needn't wet your pants!"

The men roared at their buddy's discomfiture, and the tension passed. The legend continued to grow. Where Roger was, that was the place to be.

It was almost noon on the day after the debated patrol when one of the guys passed the sergeant's hut and saw him sitting with his head in his hands.

"What's the problem, Sarge?" he asked. He figured a hangover or a headache.

"Get lost, fella. Just go and get lost!" the sergeant said. Then, as if sorry for something, he said, "Tell the men I want them here for briefing at 1800 hours, on the dot." The startled marine left, muttering under his breath.

The evening chow line was finished, and the men began to make their way to the sergeant's hut. Roger ambled in and sat cross-legged on the ground. His position had acquired some privileges for him, so nobody was surprised at his banter with the sergeant. "Hey guy, what's ridin' on your shoulder?" he joked.

The sergeant looked at him, and the men were surprised to see bitterness and fear on his face. He had been in Vietnam since Day One and didn't scare easily. He was a good marine. They waited as their sergeant pulled nervously on a cigarette.

Finally he spoke. His voice was very quiet and unhurried. "We have been ordered to take the same trail tonight for a third time. Phu Bai knows there are Viet Cong in the area. Intelligence reports a fairly large group. They are asking us to run the route again in an effort to make contact with the enemy.

"They know we stand a good chance of being hit, but for some reason it is important for us to get a hold on the deployment and strength of the Viet Cong. I wish I had better news for you, but I give you what I was given." He paused, then spoke again. "Fellas, I am not happy about the orders, but we are marines. We are supposed to be able to do anything required of us and that includes walking that trail again tonight.

"Helle, how d'ya feel about it?" The sergeant looked at Roger for his gut-level reaction.

Roger was blazing, but he knew the morale of the men depended, at least to a large extent, on what he said.

"Sarge, I've never known a patrol to go on the same route twice, let alone three times. We'll probably make contact tonight, but the way I figure it, that's what we're here for. Phu Bai must need our help, so I say, let's give them the best we've got.

"Give me a little extra distance. If anything starts, it will give you a little more time to deploy. I suggest you keep close, move quietly, and stay ready."

Roger looked at the men with critical eyes, tired from squinting into the night. "Men, some of you are replacements, and I understand how you feel. I used to be the same. You get over it later! Remember, stay with Lucky!" Someone laughed uneasily, but within a few minutes the unit had responded to Roger's positive attitude. Even the sergeant seemed more chipper.

The patrol moved out on schedule. They crossed over Highway 1 and entered an immense rice paddy. Roger was well ahead of the men, when suddenly the squad leader sent a man to bring him back.

"Helle," the squad leader said, "I don't want you on point tonight."

"Why not, for Pete's sake?" Roger asked.

The squad leader pulled him to one side, out of the hearing of the men. "Call it a hunch; call it what you like, but I don't want you out on point tonight."

Roger said, "Damn it, that's my job. Those men depend on me to get them through. Besides, if there is to be action, I want to be in it."

The squad leader became impatient. "Helle, that's an order. You take number eleven." Positions in the squad formation bore numbers for simplicity. He turned and walked away. There were thirteen men in the squad, and another man ran point. Roger was furious, but there was nothing he could do about it. Far back at the end of the line, Roger began to critique the operation of the substitute point man.

"He's going too fast," he mumbled. "He's not taking his time. He's too careless!" Suddenly, that built-in sense which had kept him alive was alerted. A shiver went down his spine, and the hair literally stood up on the back of his head. It was an emotion he had never known—the sure knowledge of disaster. From the number eleven position, there was nothing he could do. He knew somehow the patrol was in trouble. He wanted to scream, but knew he would only make the matter worse.

The Viet Cong were ready. They had laid out a sixty-five-man ambush, and the patrol had walked right into the middle of it. It was too late to do anything but die.

Satchel charges, ground mines, grenades, and small arms fire tore the night to pieces. It was like being in the center of an active volcano.

Roger acted out of pure trained instinct. He did not have time to be afraid. The early premonition had proved accurate. Now it was time for action. He knew he could do nothing for the men in front of him. They had already been swallowed up in the maelstrom of shrapnel and bullets. He and numbers twelve and thirteen were on their feet.

Roger wheeled and, with both arms spread, rushed the two men behind him. He gathered them up in his arms and, with his weight and momentum, half carried, half dragged them off the trail and into a ditch beneath some trees. With a hand on each man to steady and silence, Roger waited it out. Eleven men were dead. Those who still twitched or moved were systematically shot, bayoneted, and in two cases had their throats slit. The guerrillas stripped the bodies of watches and jewelry, quickly took all the weapons of the dead, and melted into the night. The massacre was over.

With a gesture to the men whose lives he had saved, indicating they should remain in the ditch, Roger made his way cautiously to his fallen comrades. The man who had taken his place as point had been riddled with twenty-seven bullets. The sight brought a deep groan from Roger. "They got him instead of me," he whispered in the grim silence of the night. The moon cast eerie shadows over the death scene. As he moved among the men, he came to the body of the squad leader. He paused. "How did he know?" he asked himself. He was grateful for the intuitiveness of his leader. Both had felt the oncoming tragedy. The only thing different was that he was dead and Roger was alive.

It was in the middle of his sorrow that he observed the radioman still held his set in a death grip. From the way he held it, Roger knew he had tried to get off a message, an effort which had clearly failed. The enemy had not thought the radio was as important as the weapons. It became very important to Roger.

"We've been hit! Real bad," Roger radioed. He shut down the set immediately for fear of being pinpointed and hoped Phu Bai had gotten the message clearly. Having relayed the call, he went back to the men in the ditch.

The three men lay in the mud in the ditch with their weapons ready. If the enemy returned, the most they could do would be to take some of them out. Roger spat out viciously, "God, I wish they would come back!" but the enemy was long gone. Roger was bitter.

"It took eleven dead marines to assure Phu Bai there were VC here," he said. "Maybe they'll be satisfied now! What good will it do when the Western Union delivers the telegram to their next-of-kin. 'The President of the United States of America expresses his deep regret . . . '"

Two armored vehicles and a tank rumbled into sight. Three marines were safe. The bodies of the other marines were loaded onto the vehicles, and the grim procession made its way back.

The two men whom Roger saved were helicoptered out. Only Mr. Lucky was left again. The story of the wiping out of a CAC unit spread like wildfire. Wherever the story was told, someone added, "Guess what? Lucky Roger was the only man left. The guy is spooky . . . lives a charmed life."

The legend grew larger every day. The new CAC replacement unit arrived immediately. They looked at Roger in awe. They heard about the award the Vietnamese had given him—the highest award for personal gallantry.

8
Nervous in the Service

The High Command was angry. Good men had died, and the CAC unit had not been able to secure any advantage nor to determine where the guerrillas were based.

The new unit was ready for action. "Headquarters want us to go out again," the new squad leader said. "Helle, you are the only one who knows anything about this party. How'n hell can we get out there without all of us being burned?"

Roger stiffened. He knew too well the dangers of a fourth attempt. If the third patrol was crazy, a fourth was suicidal.

"Sergeant," Roger replied, "I'll run point on another attempt if that's the order, but I like the idea about the same as I'd like arsenic in my coffee. Are you sure they want us to go out again?"

"Yep," the sergeant said. "Nothing else will make them happy. They want that group wiped out. I suppose we should be glad they feel like that, but it's a little nerve-wracking."

Rudy, a tough little Latin from Los Angeles and a

member of the replacement unit, got the sergeant's ear. "Hey man, is there some other way out to that area? Do we have to go the same way?"

"I dunno, Ferrero," the sergeant answered, "but I'll get back to Phu Bai and ask them. You guys stay put here while I try to raise them."

Five minutes later he was back. "The brass say we can take another trail if there is one which brings us out to the same position." He turned once more to Roger.

"Helle, like I said, you are the only one who knows the area. Can we get out there some other way?" He looked appealingly at Roger, hoping there was some way.

"I can get us out there," Roger replied. "It'll take longer, but our percentages are a little better. When does Phu Bai want us to patrol the place?"

"We have to go out tonight, whether we go the same route or another. It is 1600 hours now, and we will have to move out at dusk. Naturally, you'll take point, Helle," the sergeant directed.

The tough little Latin looked at Roger intently. "Corporal, you've got a reputation. I want to learn point. I'm only half your size so there's only a fifty per-cent chance I can get hit. If the skipper says it's OK, will you take me out with you?"

Roger looked at Rudy and liked what he saw. "It's OK with me, buddy. There isn't too much life expect-ancy out there. They call me Lucky, but that doesn't mean you'll be lucky. Anyway, ask the sergeant your-self."

Rudy turned to the sergeant. "How 'bout it, ser-geant? Since we have to be doubly careful, let me go with Roger."

"OK! OK! You trained for it, so you may as well get started," the sergeant replied. "Helle, run him a little back of you so you can't both be caught in a burst."

The squad leader turned to the men and said, "Some of you haven't been this close to the enemy before. This is not boot camp. It's more dangerous than general combat. Here, it's you and the enemy at close range. Trust Helle, for he's been here a long time. He isn't called Lucky for nothing. Be ready at 1800 hours. Be sure you are equipped and carry extra magazines and grenades."

The men moved out on the hour. Roger took Rudy by the shoulder and asked, "Is this really your first point operation?"

"Yes," Rudy answered. "I've wanted to run point since boot camp."

"You remind me of me when I was in basic. I wanted nothing more than to be point. When I got to Camp Pendleton, I drove the NCO up the wall talking about it. Remember, you learn more in one night here than you learned your total time there. Remember all you learned, but follow me carefully and watch. Whether you live or die might depend on how observant you are. Remember, too, the lives of the total squad are in our hands. If you make a bad mistake, I can't necessarily get you, nor them, out of it. I'm lucky, but I'm not God.

"The men who died on our last patrol need never have died. The squad leader insisted on spelling me. He put a man out there who was inexperienced. Two minutes before the Viet Cong hit us, I knew they were there. It was too late to do anything. The name of this game is caution. Move very slowly and make no noise. OK?"

Rudy looked a little awed as he nodded his head. "Man, I'll do my best," he said.

Roger and Rudy were running point well in advance of the squad. Roger wasn't going to lead the men into death. If someone had to go, he figured it best it was Rudy or himself. Either one, or both. "Certainly not the squad," he murmured. "They won't die if I can help it." In his own way he prayed.

Roger was nervous for the first time ever since he began to run point. His hands were shaking and his heart beat in a strange way. "This is crazy," he thought. "There's nothing to be afraid about. It's routine!" The nervousness got worse. By comparison, Rudy was calm and deliberate.

The patrol was only out a few minutes. Roger was about five hundred yards into a different trail when he heard a knock, as though something had struck a wooden board. Looking up, he saw a hut to his right. His reactions were immediate. He slowed Rudy down by a gesture with his left hand and, crouching low, opened up on the hut with his automatic rifle.

"Let's go," he hissed at Rudy. Together they blazed towards the hut. Roger slammed another magazine in his rifle and kept the lead pouring into the hut.

It was very quiet. Nothing stirred and obviously nothing could have lived through the hail of bullets. The men moved in on the door. Roger kicked it open.

"I don't believe it," he said to Rudy. Together they took a casualty count. They had killed two water buffalo and critically wounded three others. Some poor farmer had lost his total wealth, but the position was secured.

Before the squad could rush in, Roger turned to Rudy and said, "When I said careful, I meant careful.

Better some dead water buffalo than some dead marines. I guess I'm edgy, though. It was a rough patrol last time. I'm too touchy now, and that could get me killed."

The squad arrived to find Roger and Rudy leaning against the wall of the hut. They had collapsed in laughter. The nervous tension was broken, and the serious had become ludicrous. The squad leader was relieved to find his two point men alive.

Down in Phu Bai, a radioman took the report, "Contact made!!!" but the laughter died quickly. The squad knew that the enemy had been truly notified of the presence of the patrol.

"It ain't no use staying out here," the sergeant said. "We could all end up dead." He shot the wounded beasts with his pistol and led the patrol back to the village.

"We'll try again tomorrow night," he offered and passed into his hut for a long night of sleep.

The men did not let Roger off easily. "Mr. Lucky," someone said, "did you get your name big game hunting?" Another laughed and jested, "This is really some war. There's no shortage of meat!"

Roger took the teasing well, but took time out to say, "Fellas, just be glad I shot first. If that hut had been full of Viet Cong and I hadn't heard them, we might all be dead. They'd have let Rudy and me pass, then would have opened up on you. Sure I'm nervous, but it's the first time ever and I've been here a long time without going stateside. I'd sooner be a fool being careful than a dead fool because I was careless."

He sobered the men. They were new troops. Instead of diminishing his reputation, in some way the episode built it even higher. The area heard it on the latrine circuit. "Mr. Lucky is sharp. Even cattle are unsafe when he's around. When he's on point, a man feels safe."

The night of the cattle killing Roger did some serious thinking. "I must be battle fatigued," he figured. He did not worry about it for, by this time, the conviction had settled in his mind that he would never be injured. He believed that men would die all around him, but that he would not be hurt. His reputation had been established by his fearlessness. He did not intend to lose it.

"I must remember to move more cautiously and think before I act," he ruminated. "These guys need me alive. I can't help them if I am taken out. I'm OK, but I must stay lucky."

Night after night, Rudy and Roger led the men out. It was a time of lull in the enemy's activity. For two or three weeks they made no contact with the Viet Cong. The squad leader refused to permit the squad to relax its care. They were even more careful.

"You guys need to know," he said, "the gooks are just waiting for us to grow careless. The moment our guard is down, they'll hit us with everything they've got. Don't kid yourselves! They know exactly what's going on and are just waiting for a chance to take us."

Roger quickly agreed with his sergeant, thinking of so many previous cases when it had been just that way. He doubled his care as he led the patrols out. "They won't die because of me," he promised himself.

A month after the cattle killing, Roger and Rudy were well in advance of the squad on a night patrol. They came to a bridge where the customary canopy was missing. In the moonlight, Roger could see beyond the bridge on the trail. There were bushes on either side of the path. It was a perfect place for an ambush. He remembered his promise to himself, "I am an ambusher, not one who gets ambushed."

He told Rudy to hold while he went back to the squad. "I am nervous about this place, sergeant," he reported. "It is perfect for an ambush. I'll go around the position and come back on it. If it is an ambush, Rudy and I will take it from the rear."

The two point men went downstream and crossed the creek, then on far enough to be beyond the suspected ambush position. Carefully they made their way back through the tree line to where they expected the Viet Cong would be.

Rudy suddenly froze, and Roger heard him say, "Psst!" He knew their instinct had been correct. Carefully they came together, and Rudy pointed towards the hedgerow up ahead. There were ten Viet Cong guerrillas waiting. Contrary to marine practice, the Viet Cong did not leave a rear security. There was no one between Roger and Rudy and the enemy. They wormed their way to within forty feet of the position. They had no way to alert their squad. The radioman was always in the middle of the squad near the leader, and point men never carried radios.

"Rudy, let's get a little nearer, and we'll open fire. We've got to get them, or they'll get us." They moved with great care through the bushes towards the hedgerow until they were very close. They separated about fifteen feet from one another, working to a fixed plan. They planned to scream and yell as they opened fire. Roger hoped to get most of them, but they were not clearly defined in the shadow of the hedgerow. He knew it was a risky operation, and the knot formed again in his stomach. He had become more used to it. It had never been there until the night the patrol had been shot to pieces. His nerves were growing tighter every night he took the men out.

Roger gave the signal. Rudy and he each lobbed a grenade, taking shelter as they blew. "Now," Roger screamed and both the point men poured fire on the enemy. Four Viet Cong died instantly, but some regrouped quickly and began to return the fire.

"Let's get out of here," Roger yelled. Together they made a run for the tree line. Rudy was behind Roger. The first knowledge Roger had that his friend was hit was when he heard him call for help. Roger turned and a bullet tore into the calf of his leg. The whole leg went numb and yet felt as though it burned.

"Damn!" Roger said, but he never stopped. His gait was awkward but he made it to Rudy. Stooping, he began to drag Rudy to safety in the brush. As soon as he thought they might be safe, he stopped.

"Here they come," he hissed to himself. He laid out his spare magazines and prepared to engage the enemy by himself. He didn't have to do it. Bullets were tearing up the ground around him. He positioned himself so that his body protected Rudy. Suddenly, the night was filled with the barking of M.14 rifles. The squad had heard Roger and Rudy open up with their weapons and the AK 47 crackle which followed. The distinctive ping of the Chicom carbines punctuated the noise of the heavier caliber rifles. The squad was there. Faced with the devastating fire of the squad, the Viet Cong melted into the night, leaving their dead behind.

"Helle," the sergeant called.

"Over here," Roger replied. His partner lay bunched in pain. Rudy had taken a serious leg wound. They just stayed where they were, knowing they were safe. His own wound hurt like blazes.

Roger was at the end of his first tour. He was given another Cross of Gallantry and his first Purple Heart. His wound healed quickly. It was time to go home. He had become famous on the lines. One of the credits he had accumulated was the capture of the first AK 47 from the enemy, the first ones he had killed. He had personally killed many more. His life still seemed to be charmed. Mr. Lucky, the troops called him still.

Before he could make up his mind to take a stateside break, he received an invitation from the gung-ho, guts, and glory colonel of the First Battalion, Fourth Marines. It wasn't gilt edged, but it was a high tribute from a three-war veteran to an upcoming NCO. "Blackjack" Westerman wanted him as his personal bodyguard at Phu Bai. Roger knew he needed a break of some kind and accepted the invitation. Had he known what was ahead, most certainly he would not have accepted.

9

Operation Prairie

Colonel Westerman was a legend himself. The man had fought through World War II and Korea. A flamboyant and brave marine officer, he was now the commanding officer of First Battalion. With no guts, there was no glory, as far as he was concerned. He wanted Roger with him, more to enhance his own prestige than to gain any supposed security.

"Helle," he said, a day or two after Roger arrived, "I'm damned tired of being in this rat hole. Do you know what they call us here?"

Roger looked quizzically at him and replied, "No, sir," even though he knew very well.

"Helle, this is my third war and High Command has simply pinned me in this peace corps. They call us the national guard reserve. If I don't get into action soon, I'll give you my command and go back to the ranks."

As much as a career man could, Westerman treated Roger with respect, even to a kind of grudging admiration. "You're a good marine, Helle. Stay with me. Some day you'll make officer rank, the same way I did, by sheer guts on the field."

The colonel was not long in devising a way to get out of Phu Bai. He had determined to exit the place one way or another, so he volunteered the whole battalion to go north towards the DMZ (demilitarized zone) to a place known as the Rockpile. High Command was cranking up an operation to be known as Operation Prairie. It was to center at a small isolated airstrip near Dong Ha just south of the DMZ. The purpose was the continual harassment of the Viet Cong regulars. It was a period when the United States forces were hitting the enemy everywhere. The bombs were falling on North Vietnam, the Ho Chi Minh Trail, the North Vietnamese Army, and the Viet Cong. The tide was flowing against the enemy, and the push was northwards.

At Dong Ha, the temperatures were extremely high, and the men took a terrible beating from heat exhaustion and heatstroke. When the battalion marched in, they were in full battle gear. Men dropped like flies in the blistering heat. They began to dig in and create their foxholes, but some fell in the incompleted holes they were preparing.

Operation Prairie had as its primary purpose to stop the infiltration southward of North Vietnamese regular army units. The NVA was trying to give relief to the beleaguered Viet Cong. While it was a period of strength for the United States, it was a time of violent escalation in the conflict. The United States was more and more committed, with increasingly large numbers of troops.

Roger survived the march and the heat. During the move, he made a close friendship with a lieutenant from Georgia. Roger thought he was a great guy and began to offer to accompany him when he took his men on sweeping operations. The colonel tolerated it, remembering his own years as a young marine. Roger was incapable of sitting still. He knew an overwhelming compulsion to volunteer for anything that was happening.

From the Rockpile, the battalion had a clear view of the ridge known as the Razorback. Observers had seen activity on the top of the ridge, and the Georgian lieutenant was told to go and get rid of whatever it was. The colonel thought there was an observation post of Viet Cong in the caves, the mouths of which were clearly visible.

"Hey, lieutenant," Roger called as he saw the Georgian cross the area, "I'd like to go up the hill with you!"

"OK! You better hurry; we leave in an hour. I can use you as an acting squad leader. One of my sergeants is sick."

Even in Dong Ha, the men knew Roger. The First Battalion had control of the CAC units when it was based at Phu Bai, which was how Colonel Westerman knew of Roger. The squad he was to lead in the mountain assault was glad to have him along.

One guy made a crack, saying, "Helle, you're crazy! You could sit here all day and protect Blackjack's nose from the mosquito bites. The worst that could happen would be that you got bitten yourself. Why in tarnation do you want to go up this hill?"

Roger grinned and replied, "Marine, if I kill the boss mosquito, it will be hard for his children to bite the colonel." It was a good rejoinder, and the men appreciated the sly reference to Roger's enthusiasm to kill the enemy. They were happy to follow him. They knew he would never take second place to any of them but, rather, would lead into whatever action there was.

The company was dropped by helicopter on a point of the ridge from which access was possible. The lieutenant checked with Roger. "What would you suggest, Helle?"

"Lieutenant, this is no different than any other operation. Someone must run point and reconnoiter the caves. If there are Viet Cong guerrillas in them, some of us are going to get hurt. Let me take point and get back to you." The lieutenant agreed with some pleasure.

Roger inched his way to the area of the caves. The knot was back in his belly. He chided himself. "Come on, Roger, what's eating you?" It was one thing to challenge himself, but there was nobody to answer. He was alone with his thoughts. He beckoned his squad to move in with him at a respectable distance.

One cave was much larger than the others. It was ideally situated to look over Dong Ha airstrip. Roger worked his way to the mouth of the cave. There was only silence. "Strange," he muttered. The cave became intensely dark almost immediately. "If there were guerrillas in here, there would be smell of fire or cooking," he figured. He moved further in, and still there was nothing. Retracing his steps, he selected three men to come in with him. More would endanger the squad in the confines of the cave. Roger knew there would be bullets flipping off the rock in all directions.

"Men, it's spooky in there. Don't fire unless I give the order, and if it's all right with you, I prefer you don't shoot me in the backside!"

"Mr. Lucky, would we hurt you?" one wise guy cracked.

They entered the cave. When Roger was at least as far in as in his first penetration, he stopped the squad. His men were only dim shapes in the gloom of the cave. "Let's just hold and listen," Roger ordered.

In the murky silence, Roger and the men heard a sound. It was a kind of shuffling noise as though men were moving.

In Vietnamese, Roger shouted, "Halt! Who goes there?" No voice answered the challenge immediately. A moment later there was an outburst of chattering, indistinct but clear enough for Roger to believe it was a nest of the enemy, surprised by their presence.

"Fire at will," he shouted. The four men opened out with full fire. The bullets sang as they spun off the rock walls. All hell broke loose for a few minutes.

"Cease fire!" Roger ordered. He indicated to the men to stand against the cave walls, where they would be least likely to be hit if there was any resistance left; then he lit a flare and threw it deep into the cave.

Roger spoke first, with total frustration in his voice. "Not again, for God's sake! Not twice!"

Fifty feet ahead lay seven rock apes. They had died for a cause they never understood and in the place they called their home.

"Fellas," Roger said, "come behold the Viet Cong. Here lies our enemy. I'd feel a lot better if it hadn't happened before. Last time it was water buffalo, now apes.

"But," and Roger stopped a moment before continuing, "I'm going to tell you what I told the squad last time. I'd sooner be a fool being careful than a dead fool because I was careless. I'm on my second tour, and I plan to continue to be lucky. Just think what would have happened had they been a nest of Viet Cong."

The men nodded as they laughed. The foursome made its way back to the company, and Roger reported to the lieutenant.

"Helle, you build a war story all of your own. These guys will tell it to their children. I'll be able to tell my kids I knew you!" Roger enjoyed the banter, but knew that every man would rather be alive than dead. His action was interpreted through that perspective.

"Let's call in, Helle," the officer said.

Down at the base, from where the action had been clearly heard, a startled radioman took the message. His face registered his surprise. He looked at the colonel, unsure what to say.

"Well, what is it?" Westerman asked.

"Sir, the lieutenant reports the position is taken and is now secured. A casualty count indicates there were seven killed among the supposed enemy. They were all rock apes."

"Hell," exploded the colonel, "what a war!"

It wasn't all as easy as shooting rock apes. Day after day the position was mortared. Artillery shells kept lobbing in among the foxholes. Rockets whined at them from concealed locations in the forest. Dong Ha was nobody's Sunday School picnic. The battalion was holding for some heavy action in Operation Prairie. The men were restive. They needed action. The company of the Georgian began to gripe. "We're sitting ducks. If we have to fight this cruddy war, I wish we could get on with it. I have two months before I go home. I'd sooner take my chances out where the enemy is. At least I'd have a chance to take some with me, instead of sitting here being shot at," one man remarked.

It was a nerve-shattering time for the whole battalion. The enemy laid down a barrage at least three times every day. Up to as many as two hundred rounds would come in, and there were constant casualties.

Roger had a group of close friends who manned a mortar pit from which the Marine 4.2 mortar was used. The weapon was too big for mobile use, but whenever the Viet Cong laid down the barrage pattern, the 4.2 crew would try to get quick coordinates and send off their heavy material in the general direction which the front observers reported. Usually the directed fire was quite approximate, being determined by the flash of the Viet Cong weapons or the best estimate of the observer. During a lull in the action, Roger went to visit his friends.

The mortar pit was sandbagged, three bags deep, and the pit itself was constructed to keep out anything except a direct hit to the opening. The parapet was also three bags high and deep. It was a cozy place to hide.

Roger scrambled down into the pit and began to visit with his friends. An intense barrage commenced from the Viet Cong. The pit crew began to prepare for the exchange. Roger joked, "You guys make too much noise for me. I'm going to my own little foxhole. See you later."

As he climbed out of the mortar pit, another buddy passed by and Roger kept his running banter going. "Get out of this area. Those guys down there are going to open the 4.2; a guy could get his ears burst, just being around them." As he was talking, he heard the ever familiar thump of a Viet Cong mortar. The same unfailing knot grew in his belly, and the hair rose as always on the back of his neck. He somehow knew the round was coming right to where he was standing.

Roger crouched and ran. He pushed his legs like pistons as he drove towards his own foxhole. He had only forty yards to go. His foxhole was just outside the colonel's tent. He had covered half the distance when the round hit.

The unthinkable had happened. The Viet Cong round passed cleanly through the opening to the 4.2 pit. When it exploded, it blew the entire ten-man pit crew to pieces and set off the total reserve ammunition stored in the pit. It was a miniature Hiroshima. The concussion from the explosion of so much ammunition was so great that Roger was thrown heavily to the ground. Pieces of bodies flew high in the air, and shrapnel literally rained from the sky. It was minutes before Roger crawled to his feet. At the spot where he had spoken to his friend a short time before was a twisted body.

"That was close. Too damned close," Roger said. A great gaping hole was all that remained of the 4.2 pit. He helped to pick up pieces of the bodies of the men. Once again his life had been spared.

Roger's friend, the Georgian lieutenant, speaking with some degree of amazement, asked Roger, "How do you do it? Everyone gets killed, but you are always alive. I think I'll keep you near me!"

Roger reflected to the officer, "I don't know myself. I guess I'm just lucky." Roger pointed to the ten plastic bags holding the remains of the pit crew. "I wish they'd been lucky," he added.

Roger decided to build the biggest and safest bunker at Dong Ha. He worked for days. There was no other bunker like it. Only a direct hit from something very big would have inflicted serious injury. There was only one problem with the bunker. Its reputation, like that of its owner, was known well everywhere. Whoever was nearest to it when the regular thump, thump of the Viet Cong mortars was heard immediately dived into it. Sometimes Roger had real difficulty in getting into his own refuge. "Stay near Mr. Lucky," the men said.

The Viet Cong laid down an especially severe barrage one day. It was one of the heaviest the base had ever experienced. Roger was in his bunker when it began. Other men started piling in, until finally no more could be accommodated.

The bunker suddenly shook violently as there came a deep whoomph. The men looked at one another, trying to figure out what the sound was.

When the raid was over, the men piled out. Somebody yelled, "Run!" Only Roger stayed. Sticking out of the top of the bunker was a huge Chinese 120mm mortar shell. The hit had been direct—the only one which could have ever harmed the people inside. The mortar round was the biggest known, but it was a dud. The sheer weight of the round had carried it two sandbags deep. Had it blown, it would have buried every man in the bunker. A demolitions man defused it, and it was taken away. Nobody but an expert on demolition would go near it. "That is some baby," Roger commented. "We had another close one."

"Yep," a friend said, "but we stay with Mr. Lucky."

10
Then They Came Back

As 1966 wound itself to a close, Operation Prairie seemed to be losing steam also. The patrols went on. The harassment of the enemy continued, but the momentum, which the United States had managed to achieve some months before, was lost.

The Rockpile had become just another forward position from which sorties were planned and carried out. Some were successful and some were failures. Some were so meaningless as to appear purposeless.

Life on the Rockpile had moments of difference. Nobody there had ever been stung by a scorpion, but the results of such a sting were well known. If deeply stung, the wound was fatal. It was a common joke by which friendly arguments were ended, "I'll put a scorpion in your bed!"

Roger had grown increasingly close to the quiet, young Lieutenant Damon from Georgia. They were more like fellow NCOs than officer and enlisted man. While on patrol with Damon, Roger was stung by a scorpion. It seemed so right since he was first in everything.

When the patrol was on its way in, there was a convenient place for the men to bathe. They bathed in two shifts, one group keeping guard while the other group swam. Roger had placed his sweaty battle cap on the ground and before he completed his ablutions decided to wash the cap. He lathered the outside, then turned it inside out to repeat the performance. From inside the cap, a large scorpion dropped neatly into the palm of his right hand. As it landed, it stung, and before he could react, the stinger came up again and hit once more. He threw the thing away violently, but even as he did so, his arm was already numb.

"Lieutenant, I just got myself stung twice by a scorpion," Roger called out.

"I have never seen anyone stung by a scorpion. Are you sure it was a scorpion?" the officer asked.

"Yep, sure was," Roger replied. "I am numb from my right hand to my shoulder." The two places where the stinger had penetrated were very obvious.

"We better get you in, corporal," Damon said, deeply concerned for Roger.

As they made their way into the Rockpile, they met the colonel. Blackjack Westerman looked Roger over, saw his arm hanging loosely at his side, and said, "So what's the matter with you?"

Roger answered, "A scorpion stung me twice, sir."

Westerman was the Old Corps, clear through to his bone marrow. He never said, "Too bad." He wasn't perturbed even though, technically, Roger was still his bodyguard. He stared at Roger for a moment, then spoke. "A scorpion, eh?" It was as though Roger had committed an unpardonable sin. If it had been an arm shot off, the colonel probably would have said, "Bravo!"

All he concluded with was a terse "You'll be all right!" and passed on. As he left, Roger's marine instinct took over. He could not salute unless with the left arm, but he snapped to attention and shot back, "Yes, sir!"

Roger was tough. He knew it and everyone else knew it, but he was not tough enough to withstand the scorpion. When his whole right side was paralyzed, the corpsmen decided to send him to the nearest U.S. military hospital. There he was packed in ice and given the whole works and all the necessary drugs to save his life. One of the corpsmen was a guy named Mike Warnke. They were to meet in later years. Mike commented to Roger, "Marine, if that scorpion had stung you on the left hand, you might have been buried by now." Roger's good fortune had held. The scorpion was discriminating enough to choose the right hand. A sting on the left arm would have sent the venom to the heart muscles much quicker, before the system had time to absorb it.

A few days later, Roger was back at the Rockpile, arriving in time to participate in one of the worst engagements of the Vietnam conflict. By this time he was an acting squad leader on a permanent basis. He had deep respect for the Georgian who led the company to which he attached himself when the colonel didn't need him. Increasingly he was on active duty with his own squad, and his return was one of the vital points of his military life. The monsoon season had come around again, and High Command wanted some late action from Operation Prairie. They decided to send C and D companies of the First Battalion, Fourth Marines, far up into the north.

"Roger," Lieutenant Damon said one morning, "we

are going into an area of which we know little. I'm glad you're coming along. We could be walking into trouble this time."

The two companies had suffered so many casualties on the Rockpile that they numbered only about two hundred men when mustered together for the foray. There was much tension among the men. The operation was a typical "search and destroy" effort, and yet the well-trained marine instinct told the men that they were headed into more than was expected.

Damon sat at his tent door reading his Bible. He read it constantly, even on patrol. Roger didn't know what a Christian was, but he knew if any man was such, then Damon was that man. Roger asked him, "Lieutenant, how come you're always reading the Bible?"

Lieutenant Damon replied easily, "Helle, I've been reading it for years now. What chow is to my body, this is to my soul. When the going is tough, as I expect it will be on this operation, I get my mental and spiritual strength from this Book."

Roger knew the lieutenant was different. He held a position of great respect and esteem among the troops, was always calm, even under stress situations.

"Whatever it does for you, sir, I wish I had some of it. Ever since my patrol was wiped out north of Phu Bai, I've had this knot in my belly each time I go into action. Are you nervous when you are under fire?" Roger asked.

"Listen, Helle. It's not possible not to be nervous. It's simply a case of how nervous. I put my life in God's hands, and that is where the nervousness must end," the lieutenant replied.

Roger was to remember the conversation in the

days which followed. How well he would remember it!

The operation was commanded by First Lieutenant McMahon. It moved out on schedule. The men carried one day's rations and the ammunition necessary to fight their way in and out of one day's battle.

Roger picked the way carefully for his squad. Up ahead was a whole point squad. This was not a patrol, but a major operation. The point squad found a communication wire and decided to follow it. It was a tragic error. Only one man should have traced that wire down.

The combined companies were moving into a valley and were as good as dead men and didn't know it. The point squad found the origin of the wire. It led directly into a regimental headquarters of the North Vietnamese Army.

The NVA was ready. They had known of the impending arrival of the marines and had left nothing unprepared. The Viet Cong desperately needed a morale boost, and this was to be it. The regiment was part of an NVA division which was on its way south to assist the South Vietnamese guerrillas.

When the NVA sprang the ambush, the marines were taken by total surprise. Every form of fire power was brought to bear on the two hundred men. Artillery had been placed advantageously to zero in on them. Mortars, machine guns, small arms fire, and grenade assaults were incessant.

Lieutenant McMahon drew up a perimeter. His total resources were just a little more than one full company. There was no way out. The marines were completely encircled and overwhelmingly outnumbered.

Roger told his men, "Dig in. It's going to be a tough war!" Every squad leader tried to bring his squad into a condition where they could have some safety from the withering cross fires of the enemy. It was a losing battle.

The NVA was so intent on liquidating the marines that they sent suicide waves in three times a day. The fighting had the intensity of desperation. The marines fought, knowing they were destined to die. They spoke in subdued tones, and every man swore to take out the most enemy soldiers he possibly could. C and D companies gave their officers the word, "We'll die like marines!"

All the food was gone the first day. There was no way in and no way out. The call for help had been sent immediately and the men knew that the First Battalion, Ninth Marines, was on its way in a forced march. There were no roads, and it was simply a matter of who arrived first, the rest of the NVA division or the Ninth Marines.

Death-defying efforts were made to fly in help. Water cans broke as they hit the ground. Ammunition was the most needed item, but over half of it fell into the hands of the enemy. The little that made it inside the perimeter was just sufficient to give the embattled men a chance. Without food and without water, the men grew weak with exhaustion.

The suicide waves kept coming. Scores of men rushed at the perimeter. Roger gave his men practical instruction how to kill men bare-handed. They learned fast. The enemy poured in so fast it was impossible to fire. They were so close it was impossible to bayonet them. It became a hand-to-hand battle, three times each day. The bulging eyes of North Vietnamese Army soldiers as they died with rifles across their necks grew to be a common sight.

"Go for their eyes first," Roger told his men and showed them how to gouge out a man's eyes with two flicks of the thumbs. "You can kill'em how you like after that," he said.

Roger was killing one soldier, exactly how he had told his men to kill, when another NVA man jumped into the trench on top of his back. The NVA attacker used the same technique. He went for Roger's eyes. It was a close one! Roger let go the ends of the rifle which was choking the first man to death, figuring it would be some time before he was able to move, if at all. He grabbed a trenching tool with a shovel on one end and a pick on the other. With the pick end of the tool he swung back over his head and buried the pick in the man's back. Then he killed the man who still lay at his feet.

"How d'ya do it, corporal? You never miss 'em," one of his men said.

"Hey, marine," Roger replied. "You get them, or they get you. Take your choice. I plan on getting out of here alive. As long as I have life, I plan to keep it."

Three full days the life and death struggle went on. On the second day a wave of sorrow rolled over D Company. The Bible-toting lieutenant took a round in the chest. Already the marines were out of battle dressings, drugs, and necessary equipment to prolong life. Lieutenant Damon died quietly, with a look of peace on his face. He asked for a sip of fruit cocktail, sighed, and was gone. His men determined even more intently to fight until no one was left, if that was what was necessary.

Roger felt bereaved at the death of Damon. They

were close. To be close in battle was a closeness unparalleled by other life experiences. Roger missed him, but fought ferociously for both of them. He became a living inspiration to the men of D Company. It seemed Roger was everywhere. Where a squad was wilting, suddenly came Roger. He walked unscathed among the fire and killed every enemy soldier he could lay hands on.

"He's a crazy man," someone said.

"You're right," another replied, "but you better be glad he's here. As long as Mr. Lucky is on his feet, we have a chance to survive."

The stench of rotting bodies filled the air. "You'll get used to it," Roger told his men. "Shortly, you won't know any difference."

On the bodies of the dead enemy there were sometimes small rice supplies, wrapped in banana leaves. Whenever it was safe, Roger encouraged his men to crawl out and bring in the weapons of the dead and any rice they found. He himself gave what he found to those who were wounded, until it became imperative for him to eat. He went on his belly to a dead enemy soldier. The man's body had rice.

Roger unwrapped the sticky mess and filled his left hand with it. As he crammed it into his mouth and swallowed, he felt something crawling in his hand. He looked down and the whole palm of his hand was writhing with maggots. He retched, but there wasn't enough in his stomach to send out the maggots already eaten. "Oh, s—-!" he said and made his way back to the foxhole.

On the morning of the fourth day, Lieutenant McMahon made a brilliant move and extricated the living and wounded to a small hill. It gave the remnants of the men a better chance to stand off the continual attacks. He sent a radio message out. "Watch out for us. We'll be marching out tomorrow." The courage of his leadership was material for a major headline in the armed forces' newspaper, *The Stars and Stripes*. McMahon was right. On the fifth day, the First Battalion of the Ninth Marines broke in and relieved the small group of marines still alive.

Roger led his men out intact. As the men retreated, the NVA came after them, but they ran into a horrible rain of napalm. The marines, almost out of their minds with the five days of killing and death, stood and laughed as the flaming jelly burned the enemy to death. What would have been shocking under any normal conditions was lovely to look at under these conditions.

When the First Battalion arrived, they carried food and water. The ambushed men had eaten worms, lizards, and snakes for four long days. The sight of their relief force brought tears to the combat weary men.

Roger's reputation continued to grow. The legend grew bigger, and yet he carried it with aplomb. He was a marine NCO. The men didn't love him, but they held him in awe and respect. It was a very frequent thing for a new replacement marine to be told, "Ask Helle; he knows." Or, "Go get the answer from Mr. Lucky." When the replacement asked who Mr. Lucky was, he always got the same answer, "The best damn marine on the Rockpile!"

Shortly after the debacle of Operation Prairie, Roger had his men on patrol when he was wounded. One of his men was hit, and he went out to bring him in. As he carried him, a grenade burst within range, and Roger took shrapnel down the side of his body. He got his man in and after a few days in the hospital was back on the lines again.

He had added another Purple Heart to the growing weight of his decorations. Already he was well seasoned as a fighting machine, but there were more years ahead and the end of Vietnam was not in sight.

11
A Change of Pace

Somebody in the echelons of authority decided it was time for Corporal Helle to take a break. Roger had been almost two years on the front, and someone decided it was better for that marine to run away and live to fight another day.

He was staging on Okinawa and filling in the waiting time for his flight to the U.S.A., carousing around the island. As he walked on one of the principal highways, he was accosted by a serviceman who addressed him. "Dammit, corporal, how did you get up here? I left you a few minutes ago in the PX. There's no way you could be walking towards me! Do you have a double?"

Roger yelled "Yep!" and was on his way. Where else but in Vietnam was there another six-foot, two-inch marine like him? It just had to be brother Ronald if the man resembled him that closely.

It was celebration in Okinawa. Ronald was waiting for his plane, too. The twins began to plan how they could go together. Roger's plane was scheduled two or three days later than that of Ronald.

"Let's go and see the dispatcher," suggested Ronald. They found a hard-bitten oldster with long lists of names all over his desk.

"Sergeant," Roger said, "we have both just come off the lines. I haven't seen my brother in ages, and we just happened to meet here. Mom is real sick, and I'd like to request we be manifested on the same plane. It would be a tremendous thing for her if we walked in together."

It wasn't easy, but the two men were very persuasive, and they were listed together on a plane the very next day. They celebrated all over the island that night. The other guys kept well away from these identical twins. They were obviously battle weary men. They loomed large in every bar and did whatever it pleased their hearts to do. Nobody wanted to tangle with two giants who were roaring around town looking for whatever rumble they could create.

When the twins arrived home, it was quite an event in town. The newspapers were interested in the arrival of the pair, and for a day or so they were feted everywhere. Then they discovered the frosting soon came off the cake, and they were just two other men from Vietnam.

Following his leave, Roger was posted to Parris Island Marine Corps Base as a rifle instructor. He was only two months on the job, which brought him his promotion to sergeant.

Parris Island is near Savannah, Georgia, and Roger made the best of the opportunities to make up the long months without women. It was a riotous time for him and exciting for a lot of the young southern belles.

At the end of the two months he was called before the drill instructor review board.

"Helle, would you like to be a drill instructor?" the officer asked.

"No, sir, I would not," Roger replied.

"Why not?" came the immediate question.

Roger had no good reason—at least, none good enough for the Marine Corps. He tried his best to wriggle out of the job. The officer was sarcastic and cutting. "Sergeant, did you earn those stripes or were they just given to you?"

Roger was angry. There really wasn't anything he could do or say that was going to change the officer's mind. Roger, rigidly at attention, replied, "I earned them, sir."

The officer smiled and countered, "Well, sergeant, now we are going to make you work for them," and Roger was packed off to DI school. The chief instructor told him, "There is no way you're going to graduate from my school. The rifle range is the bottom of the barrel as far as I am concerned, and that's where they dragged you from!"

Hour by hour, Roger grew angrier. While he was on the rifle range as a preliminary marksmanship instructor, he left all others behind him. Over 90 percent qualification was normal in his groups of trainees. He determined to rub that chief instructor's nose in figurative mud. It was the kind of challenge he could understand. It was survival again, but under different conditions.

There were 258 candidates in the school and 152 graduated, among them Roger. The training at Parris Island Drill Instructor's School was harder than boot camp. Roger gloried in the challenge. The only difference was the privilege of liberty.

Among the 152 graduates, Roger graduated tenth in

the class. The old pride came back. The need to be the best, to be noticed. He never went on the range without shooting "Expert" and made a fetish of seeing that his uniform was immaculate and his ribbons were perfectly straight. He was a faultless marine. It was a matter of self-image to him, a heritage from the deprivation of his young life. The same drive was in him now as took him into the Corps and drove him so relentlessly in Vietnam.

The perfection Roger demanded of himself made him expect it of others. The common marine term was true of him. "He was one squared-away marine!"

It was now the fall of 1967, over two years since the tall, gangling kid had volunteered to become a marine. In those two years, he had lived an eternity. He was proud of himself and his fitness reports indicated the Corps was proud of him, too. The toughness of the Corps could never concede it had a great one, but Roger had become one of the best at twenty years of age.

Six months of temporary duty were spent at the Marine Corps Recruit Training Depot in San Diego. His chief drill instructor in San Diego was one of the same who had put Roger through originally.

Finally, Roger was back at Parris Island. He was now twenty-one years old. As an assistant drill instructor there was constant pressure on him to be better. It was hard because he was already as good as the best. For a year he beat recruits into shape and got them ready for Vietnam. Roger was one of the youngest instructors in the Corps.

The recruits were scared of Roger. He walked around with a smile all the time. The other instructors

were mean. Roger was even meaner when he had to
be, but always he smiled, even when he was screaming
at the men. If he bit the ear of a recruit, as often the
instructors did, he did it with a smile. It was a gigantic
act, for this kind of behavior was not part of Roger's
personality. The age-old biting of a nose was obnoxious
to him, but he did it, always with a smile. "You stupid
idiot, I'll bite off your nose," and having said it, Roger
would smile, turn the recruit's head and proceed to bite
his nose! He would still be smiling when the act was
completed. The men felt differently towards him than
any other instructor. The troops thought that all
instructors were crazy, but this one, he was especially
crazy!

"He was too long in Vietnam," the rumor started.
"Something is wrong up here," and the speaker would
gently tap his own head. In some way the men grew to
have an affection for Roger. He was hard as nails and
fair. He was a perfectionist, but he was just.

The love-hate relationship between Roger and his
recruits was to save him from serious military discipline.

During a training session, Roger grew incensed
with the ineptness of a recruit who always turned left
when the order was right and always heard an order differently than it was given. The guy's rifle was always
six ways from nowhere. Roger approached the trem-
bling recruit and yelled, "You spastic, ignorant . . . , you
blankety, blank, blank!" Roger grabbed his rifle out of
his hands, and the recruit jumped back startled.

While the episode was taking place, the assistant
base commander, a full colonel, was passing in a car. He
ordered his driver to stop and strode to where Roger

was training his men. All he knew was that a recruit had jumped backwards and an instructor's hand was raised. He never checked any details.

"Sergeant, you are relieved of duty. Right now," he spat. "Report to the battalion commander immediately." Having relieved Roger, the colonel took off.

Roger reported first to his own company commander. He did not know why he had been relieved, and when his company commander asked the reason, Roger told him it was probably for swearing at the recruit. There had recently been a directive that instructors were not permitted to use abusive language towards a recruit, and Roger thought he must be the first to be impaled on the order.

The company commander accompanied Roger to battalion headquarters. They marched in with proper pomp. The reporting colonel was seated with a scowl on his face. The battalion commander stood Roger at attention. "Are you aware, sergeant, what you did?" he demanded.

Roger replied, "Yes, sir." The battalion commander berated Roger, never specifying the charge.

The commander said, indicating the colonel, "He wants to court-martial you!"

Roger was shocked. He asked, "For swearing, sir?"

The battalion commander was livid. He replied, "Swearing my eye! You struck that recruit right across his face. The colonel saw it!"

"Sir, I did not hit the recruit," Roger answered.

The battalion commander asked for details, and Roger gave them. When he had heard the story, he asked, "Sergeant, you're not lying to me?"

"No, sir," Roger replied.

"If you are," the commander said, "I'll crucify you!"

"Sir, I did not hit that recruit," Roger said again.

It was news all over the base. Sergeant Helle was facing a special court-martial. It was then Roger discovered how much the men respected him. The driver of the colonel's car swore Roger did not hit the recruit and that the colonel had been drinking that day. The recruit and the squad testified the same, and Roger was acquitted.

Roger was up for promotion again and was to become a senior drill instructor on the base. The bitter animosity of the colonel stopped all of the action. He came to Roger and said, "They may not have crucified you, but I am going to make your life miserable." It was the end of 1968. Roger decided to reenlist with the option of transferring to the Criminal Investigation Division for training. Roger had always wanted to be in investigation.

When CID school was completed, Roger was again in the top 10 percent of the class. When Roger reported for duty at Albany, Georgia, he was horrified to find that the colonel who had pressed the court-martial was now the commanding officer of the base to which he was assigned. The provost marshal's office was just down the hall from the CO, and Roger knew there was no future for him there. He told the provost marshal, "I don't have an echo of a chance of getting anywhere in the CID."

Roger missed promotion again because of insufficient time on the new job. He cut the investigation work out of his thinking and volunteered to go back to Vietnam.

It was late in the year 1969. The battlefield called to him, and as he saw it, there were less complications fighting the Viet Cong than there were stateside. He spent his leave in San Diego with a girl with whom he was very close. He partied in Hollywood among some well-known dissolutes and then waved good-bye.

He placed his feet on the fighting field again in December 1969.

12
The Dopers and Death

The year 1970 opened with bloody war on all fronts in Vietnam and the casualty lists kept growing each successive week. From the DMZ in the north to the extreme south, the war became, more and more, a quagmire of death and despair.

When Roger first arrived in Vietnam at the end of 1965, he knew no marine who wanted to do anything else but fight and win. When he arrived back for his third tour of duty, he immediately encountered the deep, psychological changes which had occurred in the two years he had spent stateside.

There was a black cloud hovering over the forces. Men were in Vietnam unwillingly. Most of the units of the United States Army were infiltrated by men who had become professional agitators. Everything was changed. Men talked freely of a war which was not going to end and of political chicanery which kept the conflict going in order to boost the American economy. Much Roger heard had distinct overtones of disloyalty, even treason. He was bewildered.

High Command sent Roger to a language school in

Danang for a refresher course. As the school concluded, he received a summons to battalion headquarters to receive his new assignments.

"Sergeant Roger Helle, reporting for instructions, sir," he said as he saluted.

"Helle," his colonel said, "we are very glad you are back with us. Conditions are much different than during your first tour. Your experience of battle and life in the villages will be of great assistance at this time.

"The Combined Action Companies have been renamed. Believe it or not, we discovered that the abbreviation CAC was a dirty word in Vietnamese! The units are now known as Combined Action Groups, and you have been attached to the Second CAG. You will report to Second CAG Headquarters immediately. Good luck!"

"Yes, sir," Roger replied and accepted his dismissal.

"Lieutenant," the colonel said to his aide, "I wish we had men like Helle coming to us these days. He was part of the first waves of enlisted men. They made marines. What we get now makes me shiver."

"Yes, sir," the lieutenant answered. "I knew Helle when he first arrived in 1965. The first letters of his name really tell all there is to know about him! He was then, and doubtless still is, one of the finest fighting machines I have known. I expect we will hear more of him. The man is natural leadership quality. You are aware of his fitness reports. They always get better."

At Second Combined Action Group Headquarters, the "brass" was waiting impatiently for Roger. "Are you ready for action, Helle?" the officer of the day asked.

"Yes, sir," Roger replied. "Where do I go and when?"

"You are to take over the control of a CAG unit which is headquartered thirty-five miles south of Danang," the officer answered. "We really don't know what you will find. For some time there seems to have been little action in the area, but we know it is infested with enemy troops.

"Some weeks ago, a bunch of men were killed by the Viet Cong under suspicious circumstances. We have not been able to break the silence of the other troops. The men you will work with are U.S. Army and part of the unified control in the villages.

"We have given you twenty-five marines and about fifty Popular Forces locals. You will be responsible for five villages and the area in between them. Find out what's going on and get the area cleared away."

Roger walked out of headquarters and into more action than he wanted. He arrived at his village to find demoralized men. Most of the marines had only been in Vietnam a month or two, were quite inexperienced, and were not at all enthusiastic about killing the enemy.

Roger discovered the truth about the men who had been mysteriously killed before his first week had concluded. What he learned shocked him deeply. His source was a Popular Forces militiaman who claimed the knowledge was generally known in the villages.

A few miles south of Roger's region a U.S. Army platoon had quarters. Their work was within the CAG also. Each night they went out on patrol, but not to patrol. The entire platoon, including its NCO were "potheads." The nightly patrol was a nightly "pot party."

"Are you sure of this?" Roger asked the militiaman.

"But, yes," the man replied. "My family lives nearby the place they were killed. It was common knowledge in the village."

Roger saw red. When he was calm enough to continue his questions, the naked truth seemed even worse than the first news.

Three Viet Cong guerrillas had spied on the platoon for three weeks. They had patiently waited until the pattern of the U.S. soldiers was determined. They discovered the approximate number of men on patrol on any given night was fifteen. They watched as each night the patrol entered an abandoned hut and saw that only one man was left outside to stand guard.

Back at company headquarters the position of the patrol was erroneously given by radio, indicating that the patrol was progressively on schedule between given positions. The man on guard was responsible for the calls and was rostered out of the party each night.

Finally, there was a night when the watching Viet Cong saw the guard doze off to sleep. Together, the three VC soldiers were able to get to his side while he slept. In a moment it was over. The soldier's throat was cut from ear to ear. Blood gushed out as he died instantly and without sound.

The three Viet Cong kicked the door in. With their AK 47 rifles blazing, they cut down every man. The soldiers were so high on dope they were unable to realize what was happening. In a minute or two, fifteen homes in the United States were bereaved. In those homes, nobody would ever know the deaths were a horrible indictment against a generation of uncomprehending youth. The President sent his condolences. Killed in action in Vietnam?

Roger sat with his head in his hands. This was not the war he had known. "Dammit," he fumed, "it'll never happen here!" He called for a briefing session with his troops.

"I'll lay it out for you," he said. "Those men are dead. We cannot bring them back, but we can, as sure as hell, make sure no one joins them for the same reasons.

"If any man in this platoon is caught smoking pot, or is found using any unauthorized drugs, he will be court-martialed immediately; that is, if I haven't shot him first!"

Roger was angry all the way through. "Fellas, this kind of thing will not end the war quicker, nor make it easier to win. The only way to stay alive is to act alive. You must be smarter than the enemy, quicker than the enemy, and faster than the enemy! That's the way it's going to be in the platoon. We're going to stay alive because we are better than the enemy in everything."

The men clustered around after the briefing, sharing their opinions. They were divided in their thoughts about Roger.

"The s.o.b. talks like he is a four-star general," one pimply-faced kid said. "If you ask me, he's just full of bull."

"Nobody asked you, punk!" another marine said. "Do you know who that is? He's not just our platoon sergeant. That's Mr. Lucky himself. I've heard about him. There isn't a bullet made that has his number on it. He was here in '65. He has so many decorations for bravery he can't count them, along with two Purple Hearts to keep them company. He really cares about his men. I dig that guy!"

Len and Tom were lance corporals. They were nearing the end of their first tour and had field experience. Len spoke, "Fellas, listen! Whether you like Helle or not is unimportant. He's our sergeant, and he's responsible to get us home to our mothers. I am alive today because of men like him. You may as well get it straight. We're going to back him up, right down the line."

"That goes for me, too," said Tom. "Ya'll know we have got to get this area clear enough so we can live in it. I don't happen to want to die in it! Helle is right. We'll play it from the top of the deck, and I'll personally get any one of you who doesn't shape up."

When the muttering and mumbling was over, the consensus lay with Len and Tom. The marines would be marines.

"So what do we do for kicks?" one guy asked.

The platoon corpsman, John, answered the question. "One thing is for sure. You wouldn't be getting off on dope and still plan to be alive. If you're bombed out, that isn't kicks. Since I have to try and keep you grunts well, I suggest three things. First, you eat when you're supposed to. Second, you sleep when you can. Finally, you do what you're told. If you follow the ritual, you'll have no time left and you'll get your kicks out of staying alive."

The platoon began to take shape. Roger learned that the corporal whom he had relieved had conducted his command in the same way as the Army unit which had been slaughtered. One by one the men came to Roger with their fears and questions.

"Sergeant," one man said, "we've had the hell scared out of us. All the corporal ever talked about was going home. Many nights we just decided not to go on patrol and stayed here plonked out. There have been many times when the same thing could have happened to us." Then, somewhat ashamed, he added, "You can count on me."

"Marine," Roger replied, "I'll need that help. We'll keep each other alive, and we'll scare hell out of the Viet Cong at the same time. We're going to be one squared-away unit." Roger laughed easily, slapped the rookie on the back and said, "Go tell that to the marines!"

The platoon began to take pride in itself. The men took better care of themselves, bathed regularly, and ate well. Every night Roger led a patrol out. He began the process of training a crack unit. He gave them all he had, and they responded accordingly. He never asked a man to do what he would not do himself, and he always ran point.

"Hey, sergeant," Tom asked, "how come you always run point? You've got enough medals to wear. Let me take it."

"Nope," Roger replied, "I've done nothing else since I first got to Vietnam. Our best chance of survival is for me to run point. I'm not bragging, but that's where I got my name, Mr. Lucky."

The men in Roger's platoon slowly developed a winning mentality. They were part of Mr. Lucky's outfit. They felt very secure, even when on patrol. They began to kill Viet Cong guerrillas, and the tally on the mess hut wall of confirmed kills began to grow.

Roger shared again the grim story of the deaths of the men who had been led into an ambush by an inexperienced point just before he left the villages on his second tour. "Men, they need not have died! I knew two minutes before that we were into an ambush, but I couldn't say a thing. It would have made it worse. I just want you to know the secret of staying alive. Be slow and careful. Stay alert."

One night before Roger led the patrol out, Len and Tom came to him and asked to talk to him for a few minutes.

"What's on your mind?" Roger asked.

"No big deal," Tom said. "We felt you should know that we took a straw vote among the men on a couple of issues. We asked them first, how many of them felt now they wanted to smoke grass. Sergeant, we don't have a man who would touch it. You've proved the point. Then, we took a vote on a scale of ten as to the way the men feel about you. I just hate to tell you, but you drew ten from every man in the unit."

Roger began to bridle. His job was to be a good marine—not to win a popularity contest. He was the best and knew it. He could not have cared less as to what the men thought of him, so long as the job got done. Then a sense of perspective balanced him.

"Men, I was going to tell you I didn't give a damn what the men thought of me, but that's not quite true. I promised myself when I joined the Corps I would be the best marine ever. I'll go on trying to be the best. I guess I feel good about what they think. You can tell them for me, they are fast becoming one of the best platoons I have ever seen. Maybe a little mutual admiration will do us all good." Then, as though afraid of the weakness he might have shown, he barked, "Let's get moving. What do you think this is? The United States Army?"

Tom looked at Len and shook his head, laughing. Len nodded, like it was some kind of private joke. "That big lug," Tom said. "You just can't help liking the guy, but he's going to get himself killed one day, and I'll miss him like hell. Every man's luck runs out some time. He's long overdue. Ya know, pardner, if I was a praying man, I'd surely be praying for him. I really want him to live."

"That marine is too proud to die," Len countered. "I think if he were about to die, he'd refuse, simply because there isn't an established order in marine regulations to provide for it!"

13
Sex and Death

Roger's platoon was finally honed, sharper than a razor, and proud of itself. The men asked for more and more patrols. As the confirmed kill list grew, so did the enthusiasm of the men. They were really marines again. It was once more considered bad form to talk about how long was left in a man's tour. The attitude changed 180 degrees until the men were more concerned with how many of the enemy they could take out before they were shipped from the area to go stateside.

With the morale running high, Roger decided to run two patrols a night. He gathered the men for briefing.

"Men, we have become a marine unit again, and I am proud of you. I have decided to run two patrols a night. Each patrol will be made up of one-half marines and one-half Popular Forces. I'll point for one, and our reserve point will take the other."

Night after night, week in and week out, Roger's men roamed the jungles. In the beginning they were shocked to discover the Viet Cong had complete control of the villages at night. The assigned work had never been done for months, and the enemy had retaken control of the area. It began to change quickly. Headquarters had given Roger complete authority. He almost functioned as well as an officer, and the men grew to have boundless confidence in him. The two earlier tours of Vietnam were now invaluable. Roger mounted regular ambush patterns as soon as he knew the area adequately. The list of Viet Cong dead grew bigger. Once again Roger called the men to briefing.

"Our perimeters are secured. There will always be Viet Cong in the jungles, and we will always need to kill them. I have set a new plan for the next month or so.

"We will continue our patrols as usual, but we are going to run killer teams every night in addition to the patrols. I will lead one and our Popular Forces the other. We will either be back before the patrols leave or go out after they return. The teams will be three-man groups, possibly only two. You will be rotated for your turn and chosen with a view to your particular ability."

The killer teams brought havoc to the enemy. Roger's stroke of genius drew favorable notice from headquarters. The enemy was thrown into complete confusion. They were being hit from every direction and at such irregular times they could not plan an adequate strategy to cope with the onslaughts. The men of Roger's unit became more and more confident, for their sergeant seemed to have the ability to win. They had learned, finally, why his nickname was Mr. Lucky. Everything he did was successful. There wasn't a more squared-away platoon in Vietnam. Roger's personality had finally mastered the men.

The stealth of the killer teams was the factor which gave them such potency. The smaller segment of men meant speed, quietness, and versatility. Roger would take a killer team and cover three or four villages in one night. When Viet Cong guerrillas entered a village, they usually ended up dead, not ever knowing how they had been surprised.

If the killer teams ran into larger groups, big enough to make attack unwise, Roger would have the team open up with everything it carried and then melt into the jungle. He was beating the enemy with its own tactics. Down at headquarters the amazement continued to grow.

"They got six last night," the company commander remarked to his administrative assistant. "That Helle is some marine. I wish I knew how to get him out long enough to send him to officer's school. Unfortunately, he is too valuable here for us to move him."

"True," his assistant answered, "but if he continues the way he is going, we may have to make an officer of him. Can you imagine what he would do with a company? We'd end up with the cleanest area in Vietnam!"

"Now, that's an idea," the commanding officer replied. "Let's wait one more month and see what we think then."

While headquarters considered Roger, he thought of only two or three things. He thought of himself. He was still determined to be the best marine in the Corps, even if he had to walk over people to be that man. He thought of his men. He was proud of them and saw the unit as a reflection of himself. He planned to stay alive and, therefore, they must be kept alive also. He thought of promotion, too. He knew he was good and never forgot the vow he and Ronald took to become officers.

Sometimes he thought of the jest of the recruitment officer, "You may end up as generals!" Had he been clairvoyant, he would have seen Ronald's future. It was fortunate he wasn't psychic, or he might have seen his own. He was as gung-ho on his third tour of Vietnam as a sergeant as he had been when he killed his first three men—perhaps more so, since the attitude was seasoned with experience.

There was nothing unusual about the night when Roger made another first. It was just another humid, moonlit night. He had given his two companions for the killer team the instruction for their evening foray.

The team moved out of their base and into the fields. Across the rice paddy they entered the tree line and, after making their way through the jungle, came out to an open area which sloped off to the river. Roger led cautiously. He didn't want to be caught in the open. Ten yards at a time, then freeze. Ten more, then freeze again. Finally the river was in sight, with the welcome trees at its edge under which they could hide.

Roger peered along the river bank. He wasn't real sure, but he thought he saw a dim flicker of light. It intrigued him, and he signaled the men to hold while he checked out.

Fifty yards along the bank, he saw the darkened shape of a typical Vietnamese hut. There was indeed a glimmer of light. He worked his way to the side of the building and eased himself up in an attempt to see in the window.

"Well, I'll be!" he muttered.

Carefully he made his way back to his men. "There are two North Vietnamese soldiers in there with a woman. Let's go!"

When the three men were in position, Roger took the time to verify what he had seen. He managed to get where he could not be detected and once more looked in the window. He had been right. Roger had not known the North Vietnamese were as far south as his territory. He didn't know where they had come from, but all he understood was that a Vietnamese woman was apparently being raped.

He moved to his men again. "Hey, guys," he said, "I want those b——— alive! I don't know how they are as far south as this, but I'm going to find out. We'll take the door together. I'll run center point and break it in. Be ready to follow on the left and right laterals. Don't shoot my tail off. Maybe we can save the woman from what's happening, but the important thing is, I want those men alive. Got it?"

"OK, sarge," the men replied.

With a mighty kick, Roger broke down the door. In his hands was a double-barreled shotgun loaded with 00-shot. He went through in a crouch. It really wasn't necessary. The surprise was complete.

One soldier was getting off the low bed, having finished his need with the woman. The other was getting ready. One pair of pants was going up and one was going down.

The woman lay on the bed, naked.

Roger hissed in Vietnamese, "Put up your hands!" Both men had been more interested in the game than in the war. Their weapons were leaning against the wall. They were inclined to be heroes.

Both men went for their weapons. One barrel of the shotgun belched double-0 shot. In the close confines of the hut, the acrid smell of powder was strong. When the smoke cleared, the two men were dead, literally blown to pieces in the closeness of the range.

"Damn it!" Roger shouted to his men. "Why did they have to be heroes?" It was the kind of foolhardy bravery for which he himself was famous.

He turned towards the woman. His heart had hurt for her. She was, he had thought, the victim of military brutality. Roger hadn't liked what he saw.

Roger froze in the middle of his turn. The woman had a pistol in her left hand and another appearing in her right hand. They moved into a slow arc and Roger saw death coming at him. He did not have time to wonder why a rape victim was going to shoot him. He shot first.

The naked body of the woman took the full blast of the other barrel of the shotgun. Blood spattered the walls. Sex and death had played together. Sport had become sickening, bloody carnage.

The three marines took stock of the situation. The uniform of the men was clearly NVA. They looked a little further and just where she had walked out of her clothes to serve the two men, lay the garments of the woman.

She was a lieutenant of the North Vietnamese Army. Her secret assignment with the soldiers and their three-way clandestine sex had ended the lives of them all.

"Hell, sergeant," one of his men said, "I'm going to throw up!" He stumbled out the door and heaved his insides out.

Roger went out to him and put an arm around the guy's shoulders. "Don't feel bad," he told him. "I was sick after my first meal in boot camp, and this is no boot camp!"

The hut was a shambles. Roger left the bodies in their blood and led his men away.

"Remember, fellas," Roger said, "you never know in what shape your enemy is packaged! That bitch would have shot me without batting an eyelid, and I was sorry for her. That's the first woman I have ever killed, but I feel real good about it. The enemy is the enemy, whatever shape they come in."

The three dead North Vietnamese were part of a large force on the other side of the river. The encounter was valuable, for it gave advance warning of the attack which was planned from that sector. The woman was a nurse from an advance party of the NVA. Somewhere in North Vietnam, three homes got word that loved ones had been killed in action. It had been some action, indeed.

Back on base, the two men who had been with Roger made their reports in the bunkhouse.

"You could never believe it, unless you had seen it," one said. "Here's this guy with his pants half down and the other with his half up. This broad is lying naked on the bed. They all went for their weapons. Boom, boom! The sergeant never missed a beat. He's faster than greased lightning."

The men roared hilariously. It was a spicy one to tell back home some day at a stag party. Roger's image grew a little larger. The story got around quickly. "Man or woman, don't make him no never mind. He kills 'em as they come."

The legend of Helle had almost reached its high point. There was little to add. What was up ahead would only confirm what everybody knew. Roger was "the toughest marine in Vietnam."

The pacification program in the area was as complete as it would ever be unless there came a cessation of hostilities. The whole of Roger's area was relatively quiet. Beneath the surface the Viet Cong guerrillas seethed in anger. The area had been a most prolific source of support for them. Now it was virtually impossible for them to extract anything out of the villages and countryside.

One of Roger's men was fraternizing with a counterpart in the Popular Forces one afternoon when the militiaman dropped a verbal bomb. "Man called Lucky die soon, Yank!" The marine's mouth dropped in shock.

"Whaddaya mean?" he asked.

"Viet Cong offer five hunnard dolla to kill," the man replied.

The marine came off his seat as though a rattlesnake had bitten him. He was gone before the militiaman could say anything else. Running at full speed, he came to Roger's hut. He burst in without the preliminary courtesy of knocking.

"Sergeant!" he yelled.

Roger unwound leisurely off his bed. He had been around long enough to know his men. None of them would have entered that way unless there was a crisis of some nature.

"Where's the fire?" Roger asked casually.

The man came to an abrupt stop. He looked at Roger with fear in his eyes. His face was pale, and he was shaking all over.

Roger walked up to him and reached out his left arm. His huge fist bit into the man's right shoulder as Roger held him at arm's length. "Hey, marine! Simmer down and tell me the bad news," he said, gently.

"Sergeant, the Viet Cong have put a price on your head. They are offering five hundred dollars for you, dead or alive!" The man's fear was so obvious that Roger quietly pushed him toward a chair.

"So what's the big deal?" Roger asked. "They want me dead! Is that so surprising? I've been killing them off since 1965. The problem is, I keep getting better at it. Marine, you need to remember that this is the best platoon in the Second Combined Action Group. They just figure if they can get me they can stop all of you."

"Now you just stop worrying about it. Nobody's going to kill me. We'll just double our precautions and let them sweat. OK?"

The marine looked up at Roger as though he really was looking into the face of a general. There were combinations of fear, awe, wonder, and a little hero worship in the look he bent on his sergeant.

"You mean you aren't scared, sergeant?" he asked.

"With men like you, why should I be scared?" It was one of those rare and beautiful occasions when Roger allowed himself the luxury of being warm and gentle. The man swallowed hard, bit his lip, then stood up straight. He grunted at Roger, rather than speaking clearly. "Sorry to make a fool of myself, sergeant. It's just, well . . . oh, dammit . . . you see, we just don't want to lose you," he said and stepped out of the sergeant's hut.

Roger would not have been human had he not been touched by this unusual tribute and display of loyalty and affection, but he knew he could never let it multiply. He called a general briefing.

"So, here's the way it is men. The Viet Cong guerrillas want me dead. Five hundred dollars is a lot of money for a man in this or any other village. It is a great temptation, even for people whom we think are loyal.

"If I'm not scared, then nobody should be. I came to fight and if necessary die. Since I don't plan on dying, I guess you and I go on fighting. It's the old school thing of 'let the best man win,' and I figure I am better than any of them. Incidentally, so are you.

"You will treat this story as though you had never heard it. From today we put the heat on them more than ever. We kill every guerrilla we can see between our sights. The threat is a challenge to us all. We would all be poorer without one another, so we stick close, stay alert, and be careful."

Roger strode away from his men. In that moment he never felt nearer to his goals. He had become such a threat there was a price on his head. He laughed silently and began to plan the next ambush.

A week later, Roger was standing near the village fence, talking with one of his Popular Forces counterparts. Almost accidentally, he observed a villager wearing a heavy poncho. Beneath it hung the barrel of an AK 47.

"He's going to shoot me," Roger calmly thought. The man moved decisively, but before he could aim, Roger placed two .45 revolver rounds in his head. Mr. Lucky, the legend called him! It was the only attempt to get the bounty money. The man lost!

14
His Luck Held Out

On the law of averages alone, Roger Helle should have been taken out by the enemy during his first tour of Vietnam. He seemed driven by a remorseless ambition to succeed. Many times he thought of the words which he and Ronald had shared in the Marine Corps Recruit Training Depot in San Diego during the latter part of 1965. The words never left him. Ronald said, "Let's be good marines. They can't beat us unless we let them."

Roger had replied, "Only three men will leave here as privates first class. I plan to be one of them. I plan to be an officer and a gung-ho marine. It may be a long pull, Ron, but I'll make it!"

By any standard Roger had made it. With three stripes on his arm, he had the authority of an officer. He knew the day was coming when he would become one. It was a warming thought for the gangly boy from Toledo, the product of an impoverished background. To him, the important thing was that he had achieved most of his goals.

When that marine rushed into his room and told

Roger that there was a price on his head, he was both shaken and elated. He dared not let anyone see him rattled, but inside he was squirming. What the marine saw and heard was different; the men saw Mr. Lucky, but he wasn't really feeling that brave. The years of discipline enabled Roger to carry off his charade without betraying his qualms.

Roger sent for his counterpart in the Popular Forces, the staff sergeant. "Staff," he said, "there is a rumor around that the enemy has put a price on my head. I want you to track it down for me and report when you find out what it is all about."

"Shall do," he replied in perfect English. He left the hut and was back within an hour.

"You got it right, sergeant. Five big ones for anybody who can bring you in, dead or alive," he reported.

"What about your men, staff?" Roger asked. "Is there any chance we could have a rotten apple among them?"

He looked shocked, then hurt. "Sergeant, I guess you have every reason to ask, but the idea isn't to my liking. The men I have would go to death for you. Their loyalty is not in question."

Roger felt a little ashamed, but reminded himself that it was necessary to start at home first. "You know I believe that is true," he replied, "but whenever a check is made, it begins at home.

"What about this particular village? Can we trust the people here?" he asked his friend.

"Generally, yes, but you and I both know it takes much less money than the price on your head to buy some of these people. I suggest you use extreme care and alert all the regular troops. It is my belief someone will try to get you soon."

It wasn't a very comforting thought, but Roger appreciated the candor of the staff sergeant's answers. He was adequately warned.

His philosophy that he was the best marine around stood him in good stead. When Roger spoke to the troops, he was able to carry it off with the same lightness as he used with the marine who first told him of the matter. The troops were encouraged and ready to hit back with everything they had.

Roger was a little rattled by the first attempt on his life. The man whose head he blew off seemed so ordinary and normal. All the uneasiness returned. Roger braved it out, but for the first time since he became a marine, he was restless.

"Why in hell did I come back a third time?" he asked himself. "I should have stayed at home! Nobody was trying to blow me apart for money there."

Late on the day of the attempt on his life, Roger sat trying to determine where he was coming from and where he was going. There was an hour or two of confusion. Then he became angry clear through. He fumed and cursed. There would be no gook getting him. If he got it at all, it would be in fair fighting; that is, as fair as the fighting ever was in Vietnam.

He laid out new plans for the platoon—crazy, glorious plans—plans which would divert the attention of the troops, totally occupy and absorb his mind, and flay the enemy alive.

Roger called a briefing for 1000 hours the next day. The men knew there was something big in the offing. He required all Popular Forces men to attend, in addition to his platoon. It was an unusual procedure. There was an air of excitement among the men as he walked into the briefing room. Not even Roger's counterpart knew his intention.

"Men, this will be the most important briefing the platoon has ever known," he began. Every man suddenly sat up. Roger could almost see the points of their ears rotate. He had their immediate attention.

"Here on the map, you will see an area shaded out. It lies slightly to the north of our own area and is uncontrolled. The Viet Cong have complete domination of it.

"Here, where the tip of my pointer rests, are the headquarters of the guerrilla activity. The immediate surrounding area is a maze of bunkers. Intelligence reports heavy concentrations of weaponry, including some of the more sophisticated Russian material.

"As of this time, our own headquarters have not felt they could mount any attack against the place. The operations sections say it will take some months to muster the strength to go in and clean out the nest of guerrillas.

"I have decided that we will take the area by ourselves."

There was an unearthly quietness in the room. Roger looked at the Vietnamese staff sergeant and was glad to see the excitement in his eyes. He could hardly contain himself. Both of them knew there was a Korean marine company nearby, as well as various other military contingents. Their own headquarters were faced with the great problem of how to coordinate all the various segments. They were quite bogged down in logistics. Alone, they had no such problem.

"In planning this assault," Roger continued, "I am depending totally on the element of surprise, combined with your daring and willingness to fight." He risked a personal allusion, knowing every man would understand what he said. "I have no intention of sitting around here waiting for some idiot to become a hero and try to take me out. The last one failed and I don't have the time to wait on the next!"

There was a titter of laughter. The allusion was broad enough to make it appear he didn't give a damn one way or the other. As far as the troops were concerned, it was true. He determined not one of them would ever know the uneasiness of his stomach. He hadn't gotten used to it himself.

The men were all waiting for additional details, but he was not ready, not by a long shot.

"Normal patrol activity will be resumed tonight, as well as killer team activity. I'll have a major briefing the day after tomorrow at the same time." Roger dismissed the men, while beckoning the Popular Forces NCO to join him in his hut.

For two days they plotted the action. They faced together all the "what if" situations, until they were both convinced that there was no contingency with which they had not dealt.

"Staff, what are your estimates of our chances of success and what casualties do you expect us to take?" Roger asked. The man was good, really good. He never wasted words or time. He hated the Viet Cong and was committed to their destruction. His reply was reassuring.

"Sergeant, under all normal circumstances I would call this a suicide mission, for which I personally would volunteer my men. However, it has just enough elements of advantage that it could be one of the finest actions of the war. If we get in unannounced, we can take that position with very few casualties.

"The enemy wouldn't dream of an attack by an isolated platoon. If our own headquarters were planning this, somehow the enemy would be apprised and be ready. In our case, the attack is stupidity, but I believe it will work, simply because the Viet Cong will be unprepared. I say it will work!"

By the second day, the attack plans were finalized. Roger planned to use the whole force in the raid, pull back, and then make daily excursions into the area until it was clean.

He briefed the men on the schedule. The men of the Popular Forces were as psyched up as his own men. The troops could all smell a big one coming and wanted to be a part of an action which would make the platoon famous. Roger listened while his counterpart briefed his men. His own Vietnamese was good enough to know he was making capital from the briefing. He hated communists.

"These pigs that ruin our nation we shall kill. We will fight as we have never fought. Maybe a few of us will die, but the victory will be large. This marine sergeant, he is a great tactician. We will do all we can to match the United States Marine Corps." His men applauded him and he turned to Roger with a smile, saying, "The men are ready! When do we strike?"

Roger felt like General MacArthur. He knew High Command would never have sanctioned the action but would applaud it if it were successful. As MacArthur with his general's stars made unilateral decisions, he too made this one. It was a proud moment for Roger as he addressed the men again.

"We move at dusk tomorrow night. The normal patrols run tonight and will help to confuse the enemy into thinking we are on normal schedule.

"Final briefing will be at 1500 hours tomorrow afternoon." He drew himself up rigidly to his full height and laid his last word on them. It was immediately translated into Vietnamese and among both groups of men caused jaws to jut and mouths to snap shut.

"The ears of the enemy are big!" His voice was lethal and grim as he spoke. "Whichever man opens his mouth may effectively kill his best friends. Button up your lips!"

Roger knew the mettle of his men. They worked on their survival equipment and rifles, checked their grenades, magazine supplies, and bandoliers. Even clothes and footwear came under scrutiny, and survival rations were meticulously prepared.

The first streaks of light were in the eastern sky when they hit the Viet Cong. It was a totally unexpected attack, as they had hoped it would be.

Roger's men took a frightful toll of the enemy, killing every one they could draw sight on. The enemy's confusion was complete. From out of the fleeing Viet Cong they took more than a dozen prisoners for interrogation.

He was faced with a dilemma. The captured weapons reached such proportions that there was no way to carry them out. He passed the word, "Carry what you can and stock the rest. We'll come back for the stuff tomorrow night."

As the sun rose, he led his jubilant troops back. They had suffered minor casualties only. It was a proud day for Roger.

The Second Combined Action Group's battalion commander went out of his way to congratulate Roger. "A brilliant operation, Helle! We won't forget this one, I promise you." He knew that had he failed, the recriminations would have been far more intense than the congratulations.

He was humming happily as he entered his hut. Mr. Lucky! The star under which he had been born was still shining. He smelled a promotion coming up. It was a good feeling.

"Just call me Mr. Lucky!" Roger whispered to himself as he lay down to catch some sleep.

15
His Luck Ran Out

Roger had learned to accept praise with an external humility, and in the afterglow of success it stood him to good advantage. The men in his platoon were ecstatic. From where they stood, he had given them a chance for glory and made it stick. They were like so many bantam roosters, strutting and preening themselves with their own satisfaction. It was part of Roger's image maintenance program to let them think that they were the greatest—they really were some of the finest troops in the Corps.

At the personal level, Roger preened himself more than all of them together. He was a success and he knew it. The sheer bravado of the operation into enemy territory was top news on the front. He began to wonder how he might enhance what he had gained.

"Hey, staff," he called to his Vietnamese friend, "let's get our heads together on a follow-up action. We need to hit the enemy again before he has time to regroup."

"I agree," he answered. "If we give the Viet Cong more than a day or two, they will have retaken all we gained. My guess is they already have patrols into the area, and probably nearer to us than we know."

Again Roger felt the knot tie in his guts. Fear, as a quality or emotion, had been foreign to him on his first tours, and he bitterly reproached himself for the weakness that he felt in himself. He imagined the Viet Cong patrols writhing through the long grass. Perhaps the Viet Cong would hit them in the same devastating way in which Roger's men had taken them. He cautioned himself into a calmer frame of mind. The charmed life would last. He told himself that he had to make it last.

Together they planned the patrols which were destined to clean the area which they had raided. He decided to take a double-sized group with double point control.

"We'll make an early morning sortie," Roger told the men. "My purpose is to blow up the bunkers in that area and to destroy such weapons as we cannot bring back. I don't anticipate much enemy opposition. Prepare for only what you would take on a normal patrol."

Roger chose the third morning after the raid for the patrol. It was then or never. He was scheduled for a routine staff conference in Danang, and he wanted to finish the job before he left. The continued approval of the High Command would be sweet when he got back to headquarters.

It had always been his policy to do everything a little better than anybody under his command. "I'm tougher," was a phrase which was frequently on his lips. Roger believed it and that made it so.

"What'll I take?" he asked himself. "I must be ready for any possible eventuality." Roger made the written list of what he intended to carry. When he estimated the weight of what he planned, it showed up at nearly fifty pounds without rifle and magazines. It was more than Roger had ever carried. "Why bother?" he ruminated, but knew in the same instant he was going to carry it anyway. He knew every man in the patrol was already prepared and snatching what sleep was possible before dawn.

Roger looked at the array of material on the floor. It not only was heavy, but it looked heavy. He had planned to wear only shorts, battle cap, boots, and flak jacket. The weather was humid and hot, even in the late hour. By dawn it would be stifling.

Finally, day began to break. The men were on time. "Great day in the morning!" one marine said as Roger walked to the patrol area. "Would you all look at the boss!"

He felt the eyes of the men probing at him. He looked like a walking armory.

"Hey, sarge," someone asked, "are you going all the way to the DMZ?"

"Nope," he replied, "but when I'm through today, there won't be any bunkers or weapons. It'll save us another trip and let us control the area by ordinary patrols." Roger sounded a lot braver than he felt.

On his person he carried enough explosives for the platoon. In a regulation demolition bag there were four blocks of Composition B explosive. Each weighed five pounds. In a second empty D/B, which had been in his hut, Roger loaded twelve incendiary grenades and six white phosphorous grenades. He strapped a box of blasting caps to the ensemble, loaded himself down with a surplus of spare magazines, and carried his rifle. It was little wonder the men were so shocked. He looked like an accident, waiting for somewhere to happen.

It was a strange sensation to stand before his men in such a way. Some of them obviously thought Roger had flipped. He thought in one sense that he had. He was tired of the whole war, but determined to make it through with whatever honors, promotions, and credits he could amass. A psychologist would have sent him on R & R.

Roger briefed the men, who listened too intently, it seemed. He had the strangest feeling that they were edgy, even apprehensive. He quipped with them. "You guys look at me as though I just arrived from Mars, or as though I was going on Star Trek!"

The men began to settle as they prepared for the patrol. As a kind of parting joke, one man asked, "You are running point, aren't you, sergeant?"

"Yep," Roger replied, "I surely am."

"Then," he finalized, "be a good daddy and stay way up there! When you blow man, just remember shrapnel loops a long way!"

It was the kind of joke not normally acceptable, but Roger took a look at himself and realized how wild he appeared and how spooked they were by it. He decided to joke back. The guy was as thin as a rail, so Roger suggested, "Turn sideways, marine, and it'll all go right by you." The men laughed, this time genuinely. The tension was broken, and they were on their way.

It was 0700 hours. Roger's patrol was poised at the edge of a huge field of long grass. It was a critical point, a funnel through which either the enemy or they had to travel to make contact. It was a natural place for booby traps and mines. No squad leader worth a dime would take his men over such a place without the point man clearing a pathway.

Roger was running point, as he had since late 1965.

"You guys wait here. When I signal it is all clear, come on in regular order. Keep low! There is enough grass cover to give some protection from the enemy if they are looking this way."

Mentally, he just knew there was no enemy. As far as he was concerned, Roger had personally annihilated him in the main raid. When he found the first booby trap, he was surprised. The words of his Vietnamese counterpart came back. He had thought that the Viet Cong were probably nearer than they knew. Roger realized he was right, but the matter of defusing mines and booby traps, or marking them as danger spots was all routine. He marked each one he found and moved cautiously on.

"Wow!" he muttered. "I nearly triggered one." Roger looked down and froze as he saw how close he had come to springing a "Bouncing Betty."

"That baby would have cut me in half," he told himself. The grenade which carried that name was feared greatly. When sprung, it jumped to waist height before exploding. Roger was almost finished with his work and was already planning to bring the men on when disaster struck.

With the training of years on point, Roger knew that he was in trouble. He had only time to say, "Something's wrong," and then an object hit his leg. He looked up and there was not a thing to be seen. The knot bulged in his stomach. Sheer instinct was warning him.

Roger looked down, with his rifle trailing loosely in his hand. Only eighteen inches in front of him lay a grenade, pinless and ready to go.

A scream died on his lips. He knew it was too late. In the second or two left to him, Roger recognized the grenade as being one of their own, thrown back by the enemy soldier—a fragmentation grenade of the most modern type.

Roger stood petrified. When the grenade blew, it lifted him bodily and threw him through the air to land with a sickening thud. He knew he was shot all to pieces, but he was brilliantly conscious.

The terrible fear of the preceding two months suddenly crystallized. Roger knew mental agony for the first time. "No! No! This can't be happening to me," he cried out, but it had already happened. He had seen hundreds of men die, his and theirs. Roger's star had shone brightly for him. He was Mr. Lucky. Bullets and bombs never had his name on them. He had joked so often about it, but suddenly it was all wrong.

The big, brash, and brave marine was lying face upwards in a Vietnamese field, blown to pieces by a grenade made in the good old U.S.A.

Roger's whole life flashed before him, from the slums of Toledo to that moment. He even thought of the men whose lives he had so easily snuffed out. "Oh, God, what will I do," he mentally shrieked. An American M26 grenade had done in a second what the enemy had never been able to accomplish. He wondered who would get the reward.

Fear and terror brought reaction in his body. Later, much later, he was to know that he achieved the impossible. Roger got to his feet, staggering as he stood. There was no way for him to see, for there were literal rivulets of blood pouring from many places on his head and face. He reached up and wiped the flow away from his eyes. Roger's vision cleared partially to give him a clear view of a soldier of the North Vietnamese Army standing about forty feet away.

"He's going to shoot me," he thought. Roger was so terrified that his own observation was meaningless to him. He saw the rifle recoil once, then twice. He heard nothing, for the grenade had blown out his hearing. The first shot tore into his stomach; the second shattered his right arm, spun him around, and threw him once again onto the ground.

The momentum of the fall kept Roger moving until he was once again on his back. The agony was horrible. He felt as if a red-hot poker had passed through his stomach.

He was still brilliantly conscious, alive in an otherwise crazy world. Roger looked up through his pain, and the man who shot him was looking down at him with a savage grin.

It was all unreal now.

The soldier's rifle carried a bayonet which was very much the shape of an 1865 vintage American bayonet. It was needle sharp. He placed the bayonet point in the center of Roger's belly and quietly pushed it all the way through. It entered smoothly and felt like a burning wire passing through him. Suddenly the soldier was gone. Roger couldn't figure out where.

No words ever framed by man could express the stark terror of that moment. The grenade had splattered Roger onto the ground. The soldier had shot him twice and then quietly bayoneted him, but Roger's mind was virile and active.

"Why me? Why me?" were the words framed in his

brain. Roger knew that he didn't want to die. He wanted, more than anything in the world, to live. He had come so far, just a little further and he would have been home safely. "Why now? Why me?"

Roger's luck had suddenly run out, altogether out.

It wasn't over yet. He had no way to know that Tom, his lance corporal, had shot the NVA soldier. Roger knew that the soldier wasn't there any longer, but in his place came a searing, burning hell. A piece of shrapnel had pierced one of the phosphorous grenades, and the contents were spilling onto his shoulder and arm.

"God!" Roger yelled. "I've got to get out of this flak jacket."

Only the men who were there live to tell what happened then, and they saw every detail. They stared in unbelief.

Out of the grass Roger pulled his smashed body. He dragged himself up until once again he was standing. With every fiber of his life Roger wanted to get away from there. He had seen what the NVA did to wounded men. They did what the guerrillas had done to the village chief. Somehow he shrugged off the flak jacket. His bowels were pushing out of his abdomen. Roger shoved them back in with his left hand and turned to where his patrol had been.

Blinded by his own blood, his shoulder and arm burned terribly; with multiple shrapnel wounds, two bullets and bayoneted, Roger began to stagger towards his men.

He felt the restraining arms of his corpsman. Roger heard his voice as an echo from some remote and far distant past. Compassion filtered in from his words.

"Easy, sergeant! Easy does it!" Strong arms lifted him and carried him to safety.

Roger felt a surge of strength in his mind. His body was inert, but he had to get his men out of there.

Clear enough for the NCOs to hear, Roger gave the orders for withdrawal. He ordered a helicopter, commanded the patrol as to how it should defend itself if there was an NVA unit approaching, and then, although conscious, became unable to communicate further.

His luck had run out, for sure. Later he received the Bronze Star for Gallantry in controlling his men under conditions of extreme danger.

16
Talking to God

Roger's deepest longing in the moments after the corpsman brought him in was to lapse into unconsciousness. Not even the massive morphine injection which he was given was able to cope with the excruciating pain that was beginning to devour him. From the top of his head to his feet, Roger felt as though a bulldozer had run over him. He had no real idea of the extent of his wounds. His mind was clear, and every development around him registered distinctly.

When the helicopter came in, he watched it hover and land. It was a huge troop-carrying type, not at all like what was used normally to take out wounded men. He guessed it was the nearest to his position.

His men placed him gently through the rear gunner's door. Roger was hurt inside as well as in his body. Some of his men had tears on their faces, one of the few times he had ever seen men cry in battle. He was worried about them.

"We're OK, sergeant," Tom said. "You just get out of here and get back as soon as you can. What kinda outfit do you think this will be without you?" He smiled at Roger as he spoke, but Roger felt the words he never said.

There was nobody else on that big chopper but him and the crew. The rear gunner looked down at Roger, shook his head, and walked away.

A clammy coldness came over his body. Roger was an old and experienced front line man. He knew it was the clamminess of approaching death. He had seen it hundreds of times and heard men complain as it developed and the lights began to go out. Roger knew he was finished, and yet he remained conscious. He had time to think.

As the helicopter landed, Roger was even more clearly aware of all that was going on around him. He felt as if his real self had been lifted out of his body and was looking in on the proceedings. The medical personnel placed Roger on a hospital cart, and a doctor began to question him as they pushed him into the emergency area.

"What's your name and serial number, sergeant?"

"What outfit are you with?"

"Do you have any relatives you wish to be notified?"

It was the same old thing. Roger had even done it himself when he had brought in men whom he did not know.

The stimulation of the questions had jolted him sufficiently. He was able to speak weakly, telling the doctor what he wanted to know. He gave him his brother's name and unit. It was the last thing Roger could say. The final resources of strength were gone.

The doctor spoke to Roger, bending low to be sure that he understood. "Marine, we're going to put you under now and operate." He was only dimly aware of the mask placed over his face and welcomed the darkness which followed.

The doctors who attended Roger were perplexed as to where to begin. There had been no report as to what wounds he had. Roger lay naked on the operating table while they went over his body. There was the first quick look, then startled exclamations.

"Hey, Doc, look at this!" one doctor said. He pointed to the area where the phosphorous had burned out three-eighths of an inch of flesh. It was a wide area of the shoulder and arm.

The other doctor became visibly agitated, "I've never seen a man in this shape who was still alive. He was even conscious when we got him. He must have the constitution of an ox."

"Look at these abdominal wounds! The man should be dead. God knows what hit him. It looks like he was run over by a train. This wound is clearly a bullet," he said, as he indicated where the AK 47 round had slammed into Roger's belly.

"What's this other wound?" the other doctor asked. Both men peered at the clean, knife-like appearance of the wound, and one said, "I don't know how it could be, but that's a bayonet wound as sure as I'm a doctor!"

His friend picked up the dialogue as they worked. "I'd like to know how he got all this. It is the most amazing variety of wounds I have seen on one body, either in Korea or here. It seems as though the man was wounded in stages!"

The medical team finished its inspection. One thing was very clear: intestines hanging out of a man's abdomen was first priority.

It was messy surgery. The bullet had torn its way

through the internal organs, necessitating careful repair in many places. The wound of the bayonet had been precise, but every part through which it sliced required the same care. The cuts were easier to suture than the rips caused by the shrapnel.

The doctors cleaned out the burned flesh, scrubbed the base of the burn, and applied proper dressings. They cleaned the shrapnel wounds but simply covered them with sterile dressings. Roger was too weak to sustain more surgery.

Roger's condition was very serious. He was wheeled into the ward with tubes strung about his body. His blood loss had been so great that the doctors despaired of getting enough replacement into him fast enough to save him. Mercifully, they succeeded. Drainage tubes and intravenous feeding lines completed the picture. Roger was alive, but barely alive.

The senior doctor remarked, "He's got a fighting chance, that's about all. I've never worked on such a mess."

Before the doctors turned Roger over to the ward, they made a careful inventory of his wounds. They knew they must weigh carefully the order of next priority.

The inventory showed fifty-seven shrapnel wounds requiring surgical attention; deep flesh burns requiring extended treatment and transplants; one elbow smashed by a bullet; one midline bullet penetration of the abdomen requiring extensive abdominal surgery, coupled with severe bayonet cutting also requiring extensive operation; severe inner damage to the prostate area from shrapnel penetrations in the groin; two kneecaps destroyed; fractured arms and legs; and severe shock from loss of blood.

The doctors stood talking about the case long after Roger had been taken away. "Miraculously," one doctor remarked, "no artery was cut, the heart and lungs were undamaged, and the eyes can be saved. His flak jacket undoubtedly saved his life. The report said he was carrying about fifty pounds of explosive. It beats me how some of it didn't blow. In addition to what we have listed, I suspect there are multiple slivers of steel all over him. It would be a good case to write up for a medical journal!"

Some days later, Roger began to phase in and out of consciousness. His hearing had not been damaged permanently, apart from the deafness at the time of his wounding. He could see shapes and figures as they passed by his bed. Finally Roger became conscious for a brief time.

An old friend from CID days was standing at the end of his bed. He came around and put a hand on Roger's pillow. He was crying and shaking his head. Patting the bed, he said, "Everything's going to be all right. Everything's going to be all right," and walked away. Roger slipped back into unconsciousness.

Two days later the commandant of the Marine Corps walked to his bed and pinned medals on him. His presence phased Roger back into consciousness again, but the pain was unbearable. It was easier to stay out of it all.

Six days later, Roger came back again. He saw a white misty cloud around him, hovering over him. Roger thought he heard himself ask, "Why is there a cloud in the room? Why is it foggy in here?" The words were in his mind, unframed on his lips. The nurse was looking intently at Roger and shook her head sorrowfully as she walked past the bed. Long afterwards he realized that in that moment he was actually dying. Obviously the nurse thought so, but Roger was unaware then of what was happening.

In the same time period, he phased into consciousness and his brother was standing at the end of the bed next to his. Roger was unable to move to attract his attention, nor to speak to him.

The doctor was standing with Ronald. They were in conference together.

"Doctor, how's he doing?" Ronald asked.

The doctor looked at him and shook his head before answering. "I'm sorry, Helle," he said. "He's going to die! There is nothing we can do. He has sustained so many wounds. He is as good as dead, three ways at least.

"He's hemorrhaging internally, and he's hemorrhaging from both his penis and his rectum. An infection has set in which is not responding to treatment. Marine, it's a hopeless case. For his sake, the sooner the better.

"We haven't even begun work on his fifty-seven shrapnel wounds. Some of them are big enough to put your fist in. There are splinters in his eyes, neck, legs, and head. None of us has ever seen a worse hit man who lived at all, and this brother of yours was actually conscious when we got him. He's been in and out the last few days, but he's deteriorating quickly."

Ronald didn't know Roger could see him through the slits in the bandages, nor that he heard every word. The doctor's verdict had come like a series of hammer blows.

Ronald moved around to the side of his brother's

bed and fell on his knee near his feet. He began to weep. His hands were clasped in an attitude of prayer. He and Roger were only twenty-two years of age, and each was scared—Ronald, that Roger was dying; Roger, that he was about to die. Roger could not communicate in any way with him, and Ronald had no way to know how much Roger longed to do so.

Roger began to weep with his brother. He could feel the scalding tears running down his face inside the bandages. The salt stung the abrasions on his face.

When he was a boy, Roger went to Sunday School, was raised in a Lutheran church, learned about God, believed in God, and yet never had any personal acquaintance with Him.

As a marine, he didn't need God. He was tough and required no crutches. In addition, God never fitted into the life-style Roger had chosen for himself.

Now Roger needed Him. He realized he not only didn't want to die, but that he was not ready to die. It was a searing revelation to Roger. He wasn't ready to die, but the problem was he didn't know why he wasn't ready to die. Roger had seen so many die and had been very willing to die if he had to, always expecting it would be quick and all over. He certainly never planned to go this way.

In Roger's heart he reached out to the God he never knew. His mind spoke the words clearly, since his mouth could not utter them. "God, if there's really a God, if you'll let me live, I'll do anything you want!" He had seen men die cursing God. He had seen men die with a prayer on their lips. It was now Roger's turn, but he wanted to live.

It was unreal and wonderful. In the horror of the

pain and the torment of his death sentence, Roger reached out to an Unknown God. God heard him. Roger dropped off to sleep immediately.

Over the next weeks, the doctors kept waiting for Roger to slip away, but he refused to give up. Two things kept him alive: the first, an inner sense of destiny in the call he made to God; and the second, the bald fact that he was too proud to give up. The order was important. God used the latter to aid the former.

17
Learning to Live

Naturally, the months which followed the day when his luck ran out became one long blur. About a month after Roger was flown to the hospital, Ronald was still at his brother's bedside. Ronald had been told to stay beside him until he was out of danger or dead. One day the doctor walked in, drew him aside, and spoke quietly to him. Roger wondered why the secrecy, but he heard most of the doctor's talk.

"Marine," the doctor told Ronald, "I have good news for you. That brother of yours is going to live. Don't ask me how or why! I couldn't answer either question. He has defied every prognosis we have made. One thing's for sure, he's one of the toughest men I've ever heard of and the toughest I've personally seen.

"We're going to ship him over to Japan. There is so much work to do on him, and we are not geared for long-term hospitalization. In addition to destroyed kneecaps, he has fractures in both arms, three in one leg and four in the other. He will be a long time under treatment. We suspect he may never walk without crutches and generally will be one messed-up man. I'm sure he will never be able to produce children.

"As far as we're concerned, he is out of immediate danger. We'll get him away tomorrow, and you can get back to your outfit."

Ronald came close to Roger. He wasn't weeping any more, and there was just a flicker of a smile on his face as he said, "Seems like you're going to make it, brother! I guess you were just too ornery to die. Remember, I'm rooting for you. I'll see you back in the U.S. Keep the faith!" He leaned over and lightly kissed the point of his brother's nose, waved, and was gone.

It was dismal without him, but he knew Ronald had to go. Many times Roger had awakened in the night to see him tenderly watching. Roger thought later that it was his brother's strength which gave him the incentive to get well. He was a fighter, too. "Roger," he often said, "you can make it! You're too tough to die. Let's get with it."

When the nurses came each day and tore off the dressings from the shrapnel wounds, Ronald winced in pain also. Those wounds could not be closed because of the infection which was active in them. For sure, Roger was going to Japan a real cot case.

At the base hospital in Japan, he lost all count of surgeries. By that time, while he still suffered terribly, Roger was learning to live with the pain. It was over a month since he was wounded, and he had not yet eaten nor had he been permitted a drink of water. The nurses moistened his lips when he needed refreshment, but the stomach wounds made intake impossible.

"What, not again?" Roger queried each time they came to take him to surgery.

"We've got to get you well, sergeant," the little brunette nurse always said.

Roger's face still felt like a football and hurt constantly. He had lost some teeth in the fracas and looked anything but handsome. The nurse was very understanding.

"Man," she said one morning, "you are more trouble than I know how to cope with! How come you can't just get moving on this business of getting well?

"We can't send you stateside until your temperature is under 100 degrees, and it seems unlikely to get down there while there is infection in those wounds."

Roger looked down at his legs. They were filled with holes, some of them quite large. He wore partial casts on his legs. His arms were still useless, and he felt ghastly.

"Nurse, how about doing something to help the pain in my face? It isn't much to look at, but right now it's the only one I have!" Roger was working on a plan. He knew the temperatures would all be taken in less than a half hour.

"OK," she replied. A few minutes later she returned with a rubber glove filled with crushed ice. She placed it over his face and left him to cool off. He did! Certainly, it wasn't the way she intended for Roger to cool off.

His arms lay beside his body. He still had bandages over his face, or at least part of it. He wanted a rubber finger to bite.

With persistent but very slight movements of his head and face, the rubber glove began to move downwards. Roger was finally successful in getting the little finger of the glove into the side of his mouth.

Roger bit and sucked until he punctured the rubber. He didn't need but a needle-sized hole. Roger dragged the cold moisture into his mouth, letting it roll about until his mouth felt as though he had been sucking ice cubes. When he saw the nurse at the far end of the ward beginning to take temperatures, he ceased sucking.

"Well, marine," she asked, "how are you today?"

"Mighty fine, nurse, mighty fine," Roger answered. It was well that he had ceased sucking early. Had he not done so, Roger would have shown a dead man's reading. The timing was perfect.

"Why, Roger-man," the nurse said, "you have a normal temperature. We've been waiting for days for this."

"I feel great, nurse," he lied.

"Hey, we'll all be happy for you. I expect they'll fly you out to Great Lakes Naval Hospital in Chicago. This is all we've been waiting for."

Roger chuckled as they loaded him. He had pulled a fast one and didn't feel bad about it. He wanted to be in the U.S. They could kill the infection there, if any remained.

It was a cold trip. He lay on a stretcher-cot at the back of the plane. Although it had been almost two months since he had been wounded, Roger still was almost immobile. Because of the inflamed wounds which were still open, he wore no pajamas, and the nurses had thrown a sheet over him. While they were on the ground in Alaska, he almost froze to death.

Great Lakes—if there was one place Roger wanted to be, it was there! It represented home, family, and safety. His strength was slowly returning. Some of the burn wounds had been cared for, and many of the shrapnel wounds had become infection free. Roger was still in terrible shape, but he was home.

Luckily, his genitals had not been injured seriously. The shrapnel had blasted up, and due to the outward direction of the fragments, pieces had penetrated in the groin. These wounds had caused serious inside damage and were still infected. Roger knew that he had lots of misery ahead of him still, but he was home. "Be it ever so humble," he thought, wishing he could kiss the ground.

Even the bottles to which Roger was still joined seemed to be easier to look at. He had been twenty-two hours on a canvas stretcher, and Great Lakes looked good to him. Roger had made up his mind to live, and it was in Great Lakes that he planned to drive to that goal.

It was the middle of the afternoon on the day of Roger's arrival that he first wondered if the return was worth it. He had been admitted in the early morning and had been in the waiting ward for hours. Finally, some corpsmen came in with a doctor and took him to another room.

"Sergeant," the doctor said, "we are going to need to start right at the beginning. You've got a rough hour or so ahead of you. All your bandages and casts must come off and every wound on your body must be scrubbed out with strong disinfectant. We need you conscious and unsedated while we do it. In that way we can evaluate each wound."

Nothing, not even the first week, compared with what followed then. The long-term bandages were taken off. The casts were removed, and the light gauze bandages over the open wounds were stripped. With bowls of disinfectant and scrubbing brushes, the corpsmen worked on every wound. Blood flowed freely. The pain was totally unbearable, quite indescribable.

The doctor came back. "Sir, I think this man has gangrene in his right leg," the corpsman reported.

A chill went down Roger's spine. After all this, he would lose a leg, perhaps? He decided right then to fight, not only to live, but to live with two legs.

His fears were well founded. One of the doctors told his mother when she arrived that there was no way to save the leg. It would require amputation.

"No!" Roger screamed. "Dammit, no! I haven't come this far to lose a leg, too." Everyone looked very understanding, but not overly inclined to listen to his protests.

Then came Doctor "X".

He was young, zealous, and caring. Roger hadn't seen him before, but from out of nowhere it seemed that he materialized. He spent a lot of time with Roger's medical records, asked many questions, and then went to work.

Doctor "X" spoke reassuringly. "Sergeant, I'm going to take your case for a week. I'm not convinced your leg must come off. One thing's for sure: if it must come off, it must come off. They've agreed to let me have a week or ten days to see what I can do.

"If you want to know why I am involved, it's as simple as saying I care. OK?"

"Help me if you can, sir," Roger begged. "I've been through enough, and I want to live, at least a reasonable life. I've made up my mind the leg stays. I'll do anything you say, sir."

"Really," the doctor answered, "the greatest thing you can do is to keep that fighting marine spirit. We'll win the fight."

Three times a day and frequently during the nights, Doctor "X" came in person. He did not ask for corpsmen or nurses to help, but tended the stinking, gangrenous leg himself. He scrubbed and swabbed. The pain was often more than Roger could bear, but he was unfailingly buoyant and optimistic.

"Sergeant, we're gaining on it!" he exulted.

"Are you sure, sir?" Roger asked.

"Yes, I am. It's slow, hard work, but we're going to win. I couldn't have done it without you, anymore than you could have done it without me. I guess I am just stubborn enough that I hate to quit. My mother used to say I did not have enough sense to come in out of the rain." He laughed quietly, then continued. "I took the time to read through your service record, Helle. It seemed such a damned shame to lose the last one when you had won everything you ever started!"

Perhaps because Roger was weak with trying, or maybe just because he was so relieved and grateful, he couldn't stop the tears filling his eyes. He choked with emotion. When he could, he spoke.

"Sir, when I was dying in the hospital in Vietnam, I reached out to somebody the world calls God. I said then, that if He were really around, I'd do anything He wanted if He would only let me live. I lived, sir!

"Somehow, you seem to be an extension of who He is and a part of what's happening in my life. I don't understand much about it, but I really want to live and to learn how to live. Do I make any sense?" Roger asked.

The doctor was very quiet for what seemed a long time. He just kept on scrubbing and swabbing. He practically whispered, "Helle, it was God who helped me save this leg. Don't ever forget it!" He left when he had finished, without adding anything else. Roger felt like an angel had been with him.

A week later the doctors agreed that the gangrene had gone. It was time to begin to work on the wounds with a view to closing them.

They wheeled Roger to surgery. It must have been quite a session. When he was back in the ward, his two doctors came to visit him.

"You are something else, Helle!" one of them said. "We looked at what we had to do and decided the easiest way was for one of us to take each leg, start at the foot, and see who got to the top first. Man, did we ever sew you up!"

"Yeah," the other doctor drawled, "we sent for a roll of baling wire! It took two hundred and sixty-seven wire stitches to pull you together. You really are some kind of record. It's a pity they don't give medals for unusual surgeries. At least you should be in the *Guinness Book of World Records!*"

Here a little and there a little, Roger began to heal. The doctors did many skin grafts, and the burn damage began to look less repulsive. He was particularly grateful for the plastic surgeon who decided to try to improve his face. Roger looked so terrible earlier that when his own sister had walked in to see him, she promptly fainted. Out of the broken, disfigured body was appearing the semblance of a man.

Roger was learning to live again—not as he had lived, but with a certain humility, which as yet he could not define, and with an anticipation towards the future.

The paths to health and God were welded together. The directional signs seemed to all say the same thing. Roger remembers looking out the window and yelling, "I love you, world!"

18
What Price Success?

The picture started to become clear in his mind. Roger was once again in control of his destiny. At least he thought so. The staff at the hospital were dumbfounded at his will to overcome the many disabilities in his body. Against all medical opinions, Roger walked out of the Great Lakes Naval Hospital in January 1971. It had been eleven months since he was wounded.

He wasn't strong, but was getting stronger every day. The hospital equipped him with crutches which he refused to use. "I'll walk out of here on my own," Roger told them, and he did.

During the months of pain and multiple surgeries, he had all the time he needed to think about his future. In a kind of backhanded way, he was grateful to God for his recovery. He couldn't forget the words of the doctor who worked over his gangrenous leg, either. Roger knew no way to follow through on the deal that he made with God. He merely assumed that if God wanted to do something He would, or perhaps in granting Roger life He simply wanted him to live and enjoy it. He planned accordingly.

At the time of his discharge, Roger was still an evident member of the walking wounded. The United States Government gave him a full pension and sent him out on his own. Roger was just another guy who had been to Vietnam. On the streets, nobody knew Mr. Lucky. His fixed intention was to make them know that he was there. Roger used his wounds and scars with sensational success among women. By the time he was through explaining by demonstration, he was where he planned to be. Usually it was in bed. The recency of the wounds seemed to bring out such sympathy and maudlin interest. Women went crazy to look at his wounds.

Roger's sexual prowess was greater than at any time in his life, and he used it to his advantage. The doctors thought that Roger was sterile, but for sure he wasn't impotent.

One female contact led Roger to the Pinkerton Detective Agency in quest of a job. He had been a very good investigator in the Marine Corps during his two years stateside. He began to dream of the social status that he could achieve as a top "Private Eye."

The personnel boss looked at him with a jaundiced eye. Roger was limping and carrying a cane. His right arm was only partially mobile. He took Roger's application and filed it among a bunch of papers. He never intended to look at it again.

Roger's girlfriend went to the manager of the agency. "I know this man," she said. "He was a top investigator in the Marine Corps, a totally dedicated man. He'll make a great employee for us." The manager sent for the director of personnel. "Bring me the application of Roger Helle," he ordered.

When the manager was finished studying the application, he called Roger and said, "You're hired!" Roger was away and flying. It was his kind of life. He was carrying a gun again. His ego rose with the challenge.

He gave it his best marine effort. The management was startled at the immediate increase in business and the number of cases solved. The sun was up and shining for him.

In June 1971 Roger was asked to open a new Pinkerton Agency in Fort Wayne, Indiana. He was making it quickly. Since he was quite indiscriminate about how he got his business and ruthless in the manner in which he solved his cases, management began to ask Roger to participate in major investigations out of his own area.

"Helle," an organized crime stooge said to him, "you come near this case and you'll end up dead!"

"Man, listen to me," Roger said. "I've been dead already! What do you think being dead means to me? I've killed more men than you've ever cussed at . . . and you threaten me? Go get lost. I'll get you and your bosses." Roger got them, but not before they tried to take him out by running his car off the road.

It was exciting for Roger. He had laid down one war to take up another. This one paid better, was generally less risky, and had all kinds of opportunity for him to be promoted. "I'll be a general yet!" he laughingly told himself.

He was running point again. In many cases, the instincts of Vietnam were to prove invaluable to Roger and to the company. The management discovered the persuasive powers that he had, the ones which made him a leader of men in battle. He became a strong-arm for them.

Roger's work gave him limitless opportunities for

his earlier gung-ho mentality. He really felt good about his job. It became an endless line of society parties, booze, and women. It was the fast-paced life he had loved before. Roger was very content in his luxury mobile home, a bachelor with no lack of feminine company, a man who had both a private and a public life. Only his favorite girls and his bosses had his phone number.

One morning Roger walked into the largest bank in the city for a business interview with the vice-president. As he waited, his eye caught two pretty secretaries, and he struck up a conversation with them. The nearest girl was engaged to be married. Her diamond sparkled on her finger. It was a challenge to Roger. "When are you getting married?" he inquired. When she told him, he chided her. "You don't want to get married. You better think again before it's too late!"

A voice came from behind, "Don't let him talk you out of it." Roger turned and there sat a demure, pretty little lady. She wasn't Roger's type. He knew it instinctively. His gals were the easy-going and easy-give type. Many of them were from influential circles, but his prerequisite was that they be amoral. This one? Well, she was quite different from those Roger knew. He could not imagine her in a swinger's club or at a disco. He started to talk to her. She drew him and he couldn't understand why.

After a few minutes, Roger decided to take the plunge. "How about a drink after work?" He was totally surprised when she agreed to go out with him. Girls had ceased to excite him, other than for sexual purposes, but Roger found himself really excited at her consent. They made an arrangement to meet at his favorite swinging single's bar. Roger made sure that he was there early enough to put away a double shot.

When Shirley Metzger walked into the bar, no one was more shocked than Roger. For some reason he had thought that she would stand him up. He rose quickly to meet her. She was even sweeter than when he had seen her during the day—not at all like the women he played and ran with. Roger's women never knew when they had him. If he wanted to play one against the other, he would plead surveillance duty on a case and then take his choice. "I can't do it with this one," Roger reflected, as he showed her a seat. "This one is real!"

He began to date Shirley. Many years later, he heard her remark that she thought he was a horrible creep, smug and overbearing, when they first met.

As they got to know one another better, Roger discovered that she loved to drink and grew more open when she was drinking. He introduced her to his party set, and they spent many great times together. Roger's problem was an insatiable appetite for women, and he was unable to confine himself to this very high-principled girl. He often took her home after a date, called one of his girls, and said, "Let's get it on. Come on over." Roger was living a double life, but that side of him was purely physical. Shirley's standards were higher than he had ever experienced. She was a new battle that he felt compelled to win.

Their engagement deepened the relationship. They met in October 1971 and, on September 9, 1972, were married. Marriage elevated his personal ambitions. Roger told Shirley, "Fort Wayne is not a big enough city for my capability. I do not expect we will be here more than a year or so."

Roger was driving for his general's star. The price had been great. Morally, he was bankrupt. He had swung into a life-style totally alien to the morality of decent people. Roger's work enabled him to maintain the tough-guy stance which had been so important to him from the day he entered the Marine Corps Recruit Training Depot in San Diego in 1965.

Roger was once more the macho man. Everybody and everything had to yield to his power. He had determined to climb the ladder to the very top. The next stop was Omaha, Nebraska. Roger began work as an assistant manager of investigations on his twenty-fifth birthday.

His ambition was so ruthless that it impaired his marriage within six months. Roger's dedication to danger and excitement kept Shirley in constant tension. She wanted him home occasionally.

"Roger, can't you stay home with me tonight?" she once asked him. He exploded.

"No! Damn it, no. You know this case is important to me. If I'm to get where I want to go, I've got to win every one. Get that into your dumb head, will you?"

He was becoming more and more irritable. Shirley was as sweet as a sweetheart could be, but he was a man driven by inner urges he couldn't control. Shirley was getting in his way.

Frequently she tried to calm him when he was in his violent moods, but Roger withdrew in anger on every occasion. They were headed for disaster, and he knew it. Somehow he never cared.

After one bitter exchange, Shirley asked, "Roger, do you think we could go to a pastor and talk? We need help."

The idea enraged him. "Pastor be damned," he said. "Go if you want to. It's your problem, not mine." His constant unfaithfulness to her made him guilt oppressed, but Roger tried to make himself feel better by making her feel worse. He had succeeded at everything else, but he was failing in his marriage. Shirley did everything possible to please him. Roger knew that she loved him, and he could not accept the reality of it. He persuaded himself that she was disloyal to him, not recognizing that he was projecting his own infidelity. Roger made her life a living hell.

In early 1974, a dark cloud came over his life. Severe and potentially crippling arthritis began to set into Roger's legs. The doctors said there was nothing that could be done for it. It was the end result of the massive wounds on his legs and in the bones from his hips downward.

"You will probably be totally crippled within two years," the doctor said.

Roger was so proud. He wouldn't give up. He struggled through each day and came home at night to make Shirley even unhappier. Both of them began to make separate circles of friends and to drink heavily. Roger still wanted to be a good husband, as he had longed to be when he married her; yet he was incapable of stemming the tide of his own delinquency. Often he looked at Shirley and grieved, but Roger would never admit it to her. It was hard to admit it to himself. Their emotional life systems were failing totally. They struggled to keep up a front for society, but failed increasingly. They wounded one another constantly—he by intention, Shirley less so.

Roger never knew how the preacher discovered his

home. Few people knew where they lived. Into the middle of their misery strode one of the most radiant men Roger had ever known. He arrived at the door as Shirley and Roger were in the middle of a rending, verbal fight. Roger saw him coming up the drive and panicked.

"God!" he said blasphemously. "The preacher is coming up the drive." Suddenly they were the perfect, loving, domestic American couple.

"How lovely of you to visit us, sir! Do come in. It is a pleasure to have you in our home." His words reeked with his own hypocrisy. Shirley and Roger sat with their arms around one another and gave their attention to the visitor.

He started right in. "We have a special young married group starting. It is to study an important book by one of our writers. I want to encourage you to attend. Will you?"

They were not sure about that, but somewhere during the evening Roger told him about the condition of his legs. The preacher smiled very gently and said, "We believe in divine healing, too."

Roger replied, "That's very nice!"

The visitor answered, "I will ask God to heal your legs."

Next morning, when Roger got out of bed, he was dumbfounded to discover that there was no pain in either leg. All he could figure was, "He must pray powerful prayers!" He gave no great thought to the matter, except to connive and plan how to convince the pension board that they were still very bad. Roger wanted his pension.

In July, Shirley and Roger allowed themselves to be talked into attending a family life seminar. It was a ten-week course and made absolutely no difference to them, except to reveal that there were many people who were much happier than they. Those people were real and honest. Roger had to make a decision about the class and himself.

With complete understanding, he chose to turn his back on God, whom he now knew to be for real. God was not unknown anymore, but Roger did not want Him.

By Thanksgiving 1974, conditions were worse than at any time in the life of their marriage. Roger was buried in his work, saturated in his sin, and intolerant of his own and his wife's sorrow. Shirley discovered his unfaithfulness, confronted him with it, and in a terrible scene they separated. Shirley took the cat; Roger took the dog.

He did right by his wife. He bought her new furniture and put her in a beautiful apartment. Roger's life was barren. Every night he sat gloomily by his stereo, like a little lost boy.

Roger also had a stereo in his car. Often he played a rock tape from *Jesus Christ Superstar.* There was a part in the tape which always challenged him. The words haunted him. In the evenings he played the record of a song which was sung at their wedding.

Roger had achieved success. He was already marked for the top, and the world seemed to be at his feet.

There was just one problem. He had lost the only person he had ever loved. Roger tried to comfort himself with the hope that Shirley was also lonely. He even arranged for a cute puppy to be sent to her. He wanted her to be happy.

He was the loneliest man in Omaha. All the success meant nothing to Roger. He wanted nothing more in life than to have her back.

He discovered how much a man could love. His misery was real. It was accentuated by the fact that he knew beyond a doubt the faults were all his.

For the first time since the last great knot was tied in his belly, in the seconds before he was wounded in Vietnam, a new knot came.

Roger was scared, ashamed, and desperate.

19
The Tide Turns

It had been a long day at the office and especially trying to Roger's patience. There was nothing that he could do to get Shirley out of his mind. His nerves were frayed. He decided to hustle in a single's bar. After all, he was single, he reasoned.

During the day, some guy whom Roger knew very well decided to make a pass at Shirley. As he learned it afterwards, the man invited Shirley to go out and have a drink with him. The news of her separation from Roger was all over town, and many guys were beating on her door. For this one, she agreed.

The man picked her up, and as they drove away from her office, he suggested that they drink in what proved to be the same bar to which Roger planned to go. They arrived before he did. When Roger arrived later, his blood ran cold in his veins.

"How could she?" was the first thing which entered his mind. She was sitting in a corner, chatting confidentially to her partner when Roger walked in. He pulled up short in his stride and prepared to move in and take the guy apart. There were flecks of blood in Roger's eyes. He was insanely jealous. He would not have felt any sorrow in beating the man to a pulp, and yet somehow he was restrained. A power bigger than his was exerting itself.

Bitter and angry, he turned on his heel and walked out. Roger's eyes had locked with those of Shirley. She saw him turn and go, and she knew how angry he was.

"The creep with the Corvette," Roger named him. The following week there was a prestigious ski club dance. Roger had never been to previous dances at this club, but a friend insisted, "Come on, Roger, let's go to the dance. You can pick a girl, or two, or whatever! Forget Shirley; there are more fish in the sea than ever came out of it." He agreed to go.

They made their entrance a little late. Seated in a conspicuous place was "the creep," with Shirley. The man made some snide remark about Roger's arrival, loud enough for him to overhear. Once again the blood rushed to Roger's head, but his friend steered him away, and they began to prowl.

Roger felt a touch on his arm and, turning, confronted Shirley. She had left her escort and obviously wanted to talk with him. He stared her down and turned on his heel, leaving her where she stood.

Four times during the evening she tried to get Roger to talk. He was violently angry and madder than a hornet at himself. She looked absolutely stunning, and he ached all over for her. The same pride which had run Roger's life made him turn his back on her every time she tried to talk to him.

"If she tries one more time, I'll bawl like a baby," he told himself. Roger was staying in the place, not to torture her, but to punish himself. He was near the breaking point. He wanted her so badly, and his pride was almost gone. Would she try again?

"Roger," she whispered behind him, "I just wanted to say thanks for the puppy. You look so lonely I just had to try again."

He grabbed her by the arm and said, "Let's get out of here." They never looked back at Mr. Creep, but checked their coats out and left.

"Your place or mine?" he asked.

"Mine is nearer," she replied.

It was an awkward, difficult evening. It was clear to him that Shirley did not want him to stay, but somehow Roger finished spending the night. They talked but said little of consequence.

In the morning, Roger and Shirley decided to go window shopping in the nearby shopping mall. It had always been one of their most relaxing pursuits. They walked hand in hand, but the wall was a mile high. He felt she was doing him a special favor, and of course she was. She had cultivated a wide circle of new friends and seemed relatively content, although she had told him the previous evening, "I will always love you, Roger!"

He knew what she meant. She might just as well have added, "But I won't live with you the way you are." She felt compassion for Roger, knowing he was destroying all that was best in life in the chase after his career.

They were approaching the huge mall when Shirley hit him, right between the eyes.

"Roger, the only way our marriage is going to work is for us to achieve spiritual harmony together. We need common goals."

He mumbled, "I know," and became strangely

quiet. He would never forget that moment. It was much the same feeling as when the North Vietnamese soldier ran his bayonet through his belly. Her words burned like fire.

Roger knew that she was right, because the only time their marriage was anything like normal was the period when they had attended group studies during the family life seminar. He remembered how different the people were. They had fun, laughed a lot, embraced one another, and, above all, had happy marriages. He knew that Shirley was right.

He had never seen the same qualities in the bars or among the fast set with whom he associated. They were superficially happy while they drank or engaged in sexual encounters, but there was always a great emptiness left afterwards.

Both Shirley and Roger had dates scheduled for that evening. Shirley was to be with the same man—the creep with the Corvette. She elected to keep her date at an exclusive ski club group. Roger decided to break his and get drunk.

At the ski club party, the joke of the night was repeated over and over. "Hey, watch out! Roger's coming." The laughter was all at Roger's expense. Fortunately, there was no way for him to know. He was sitting in his single's bar getting plonked.

Every half hour Roger called Shirley's apartment. She had come in fairly early and was listening to music with her friend. When he left, she finally answered Roger's next call. The earlier ones she had ignored.

"Can I come over?" he asked.

"I guess," she answered, without much enthusiasm. He found her emotionally drained. The strain was catching up on her, too.

Next morning after he had showered, Roger walked out into the kitchen and said, "Honey, let's get married! I love you, and there is nothing in life without you. We know what we have to do, so why don't we just do it now?" Roger wanted his life with Shirley restored. For the period of separation, he had felt sad, and alone. He was willing to make the adjustments necessary for their marriage to be meaningful again.

Like two little children, Roger and Shirley approached God. They did not really know what to do, or what to say. In the simplest way possible, Roger prayed, "God, please take over our lives. We can't do it without you!"

A great peace came into Roger's heart, and spilled over to Shirley. Roger felt good, and in some way, relieved of a great weight. It was a new experience for both of them, but in the quietness of the aftermath, it was consciously real.

Shirley and he were not quite sure of the actual extent of their love toward one another. They had both suffered pain and inner hurts, and they did not know whether they could make their relationship work. Neither of them knew the vast difference which faith could make. They were to find out.

Roger found out the difference in himself quickly. It happened in a twofold way which left no doubt in his mind that he was not the same Roger Helle.

On the job, Roger had been known as the man with the dirtiest mouth in the company. Nobody really cared. There was no way to knock success, and Roger was successful. From the Sunday morning that he and Shirley made their decision to commit their lives to God, and to follow Jesus Christ, Roger could no longer curse. Where normally he would rip the office apart, he spoke gently, or never answered back at all. That was not Roger Helle. He was tamed.

"What's the matter, Roger?" one of the men asked. "Are you sick today?"

Through all his adult life, Roger had taken pride in his courage. Now, it was on the line. "No, but I am different," he replied. "Yesterday, I made a decision to let God take over my life. I became a Christian. My wife and I are together again, and we are determined to live for Jesus Christ. We have a new peace together."

If every employee had dropped dead it would not have been more quiet than in that moment. Someone rustled papers; another coughed in the uncanny silence.

"Did you say 'a Christian?'" the original questioner asked.

"That's what I said," Roger replied, "and I meant it."

The man looked at him witheringly, and spat out, "Then guess how long you'll last around here. I'm your superior, and I'll be damned if I'll work with a mealy-mouthed, Bible-quoting investigator. One of us will have to go for sure."

Roger felt a great compassion for the man. He thought of all the struggles in his own life. When he spoke, it was in quietly modulated words. "If it means I have to choose between my happiness and my job, then the job will have to go. But I want to give you fair warning. My job is important to me, and I plan to keep it. As a matter of fact, I plan to double my output. If you want to try to catch up with me . . . be my guest."

From that day the flak started. Roger didn't have an

emotional flak jacket, but he did have a shining, new faith, and the faith carried him through each testing day.

Every day was a personal excitement. He felt a mounting happiness. The staff thought he was crazy. Every night he had drunk with them in a local booze-stop; now he drank no more. His investigations went well, and solutions came quickly for him. Finally, some of the other investigators decided to try to frame him out of a job.

The charge was leveled that Roger was often drunk on the job, talking matters of confidence in front of clients. It began as an interoffice war. The persecution had really begun. Roger was sorely puzzled, and in his concern called out to God. "Hey, up there!" he cried out; "I don't know what's going on. Please help me!"

It seemed to Roger that he heard a voice which spoke clearly to his heart, "Roger, I want you to learn to love those who hate you. Remember, they hated me, too." For six long months in 1975, he was under enemy fire again. It was almost unbearable.

Finally, the word was out. The top regional manager was coming to Omaha to make a personal investigation of the charges and complaints against Roger. His one remaining friend in the office alerted him, "Roger, I thought you ought to know." The man never offered to tell Roger how he knew of the pending visit, but Roger took it kindly that he had been warned.

The local manager was scared. He had not figured on anything so exhaustive. To Roger, it was simple. The scandal was false and the charges were stupid. Neither would jell with the record of his work. Top management, however, had determined to unearth the truth for itself.

The investigation lasted a full week. Secretaries, guards and investigators were all called in for conference. The air became very tense in the Pinkerton Agency. The office premises were not permanent, and Roger's personal office was a small cubicle, far in the rear. The men who had tried to railroad Roger on account of his stand for Jesus Christ, had gone out of their way to make his life unhappy—little things, like pouring beer on his desk and papers. All these things came out in the investigation. The agency did a good job of investigating itself.

At last it was over. Most of the staff thought the brass would go back to Des Moines and bring down their finding later. They did that, but before leaving, they shook Roger's composure.

The intercom buzzed on his desk. Roger picked it up, and was startled to hear the regional manager say, "Come on in here, Helle." He was quite sure they were about to fire him. He slipped in a quick prayer for peace and poise and made his way to the conference room.

"Helle, can you run this office?" the man asked.

It was no time for boasting, but the office was a shambles, and Roger knew it. If he had run his platoon in Vietnam the way the Omaha Pinkerton Agency was run, the men of the platoon would all have been dead. Roger thought quickly, and opted for the truth.

"Sir, I think I can do a better job than has been done so far," he replied.

"Helle, you hang in here until next week. Keep your ideas and thoughts to yourself," the man said. It was the end of the conversation. Roger had not the slightest idea what was in the oven, but he left the room determined to get on with his own job. The question had been unsettling, but hard work would take care of that problem.

The following week, the management staff arrived again. They descended in a way which reminded Roger of one of his own killer raids. They swooped in and fired every man in the place, except Roger. They paid the men their final checks, took their keys, and for them it was all over.

Roger was exonerated! During the months of testing, God had made clear to Roger the need to trust Him. God's Spirit had whispered, "If you will humble yourself, I will defend you, and no harm shall come to you."

The men from Des Moines called Roger into conference and gave him the office keys. "It's your office, Helle," they said, and left him alone with his thoughts.

Roger knew some apprehension, for he was asked to start in from nothing, working over territory which was badly messed up and eroded. He felt momentary weakness, but after some thought, he began to think positively again. "I can do it," he declared.

The date was August 6, 1975. It was almost Roger and Shirley's third wedding anniversary. Their faith in Jesus Christ was nearly nine months old. There were big challenges ahead.

Roger went home that night with his knees shaking. Until this time, the developments would have given him personal pride, and he would have seen them as representing a major promotion toward his general's star. Now, Roger's mind grew humble and quiet. He saw clearly the way in which he had been led. His mind went back to the grim moment in Vietnam, when, out of his dying desperation, he said, "If you'll let me live, I'll do anything you want." It had taken four years for Roger to become fully aligned with God.

A month after his promotion, friends from church came to Roger and said, "We feel you are the man God wants for the direction of a teenage rehab program on the streets of this city." If they had come earlier, Roger would never have gotten released from Pinkerton to do such work. Now he was the boss, and there was no reason to refuse to take the responsibility.

The pathway to the future was opening. A stronger hand than his was steering Roger's life, distinctly and clearly.

20
Running Point Again

Shirley and Roger began to feel a strong call of God upon their lives. Roger remarked to his wife, "There must be some special work God has for us. Why else would He have led us in the way He has." Shirley agreed.

Together, they determined to consolidate their lives, and to make them count for God in both business and personal ways. They began to pray with new intensity, giving more and more of their time to the interests of Christian work. Most of their energy was diverted into helping kids on the streets of Omaha.

"Sweetheart," Roger said to his wife one evening, "whatever God has for us in the future will be helped by our success now. I believe I have to make the agency the best Pinkerton has."

With this goal in mind, Roger began to bring the agency into full production. He determined to wipe out the existing problems in the office and gear up to make the case load greater, and more successful. He faced employee problems, zero-growth problems, and customer-relation problems. There was no area of the agency which did not need to be revamped. Roger saw it as similar to a regrouping of the battlefield troops. He decided to call a meeting of the few office staff members, and those men whom he had begun to hire. It was quite a meeting.

"I want all of you to listen to me. I have a story I want to share with you," he told them. He spoke to them of his life as a marine, and his driving, remorseless ambition. He spoke of his near death and what he had promised God as he was supposedly dying. He told them of his struggles in marriage, and then, as they least expected it, Roger spoke of what personal faith in Jesus Christ meant to him. The air grew heavy as he continued.

"If you are wondering why I am sharing all this with you, the answer is plain. I still want to be the best, but now I want to be the best there is for other reasons, and for other people. I still want my general's star, but only as a means to assist others who are in need.

"This office is going to be the best in the Pinkerton organization. I want each of you to know that we will work harder than we have worked at anything in our lives. There will be no loose ends in this operation. At the same time, I want you to know I will be there backstopping each one of you.

"In Vietnam, I always ran point. I am going to run point again, and I will not ask any man or woman to do anything I cannot, or would not do. I will set the pace for the agency, and all I ask is that you follow me. Let my previous experience be the way in which you learn. Remember, the stragglers get picked off. Stay close to me, and I'll try to lead you safely.

"If there is any person who feels unable to function

in this way, this is the time to tell me. I will arrange your transfer to another office. Or, you can resign if you wish."

When Roger finished, the staff melted away. They had much to think about, but Roger did not really expect to lose any of them. He calculated correctly. One by one they came to him with independent decisions. "You can count on me, Roger." The team was away and running hard.

Business boomed! New clients began to seek them out, and they required less and less solicitation. By the end of the first year of Roger's administration, the volume of business had doubled. The year 1976 was a banner year for the Omaha Pinkerton Agency.

The reputation of the Omaha office and its associated personnel began to be talked about across the entire country. Office managers from other areas came to see what made Roger tick. When they came, they always saw a team of happy men and women, and an office which ran smoothly without tension. The vice-president of security said to Roger, "Helle, this is a model operation. I have big plans for you with Pinkerton."

Roger's excitement was real. It was thrilling to be out in front once more. His attitude was not as it would have been in other years, however. He gladly gave the credit to God. This was running point in a way he had never experienced before.

The battle on the streets was being won, too. On the streets of Omaha, the Lighthouse Ministry was effectively reaching bruised and lonely teenage kids. This was running point in still another way. It was dangerous in different ways. In these days, whatever

Roger did seemed to be in a pioneer setting.

In the middle of all the success, something appeared to be slowing down Roger's life. Business was still booming and the street work was doing just fine, yet Roger grew restless. He was most concerned that his life not become an endless drag. He wanted to have zest all the time, yet this important commodity seemed to be eluding him. He decided to make a visit to his pastor. From the first time that man came up his drive, Roger had increasingly respected his opinion.

"Pastor," he opened, "we seem to be winning in every way. Yet, I personally feel inadequate and powerless. I notice this especially in working with the kids off the streets. What do you think could be wrong? Is there something lacking in me?"

The pastor was a man filled with spiritual power. Eighteen months before he had convinced Roger and Shirley to take a course of study which continued through a family-life seminar. Roger had not understood much of the teachings in those earlier days. He remembered the classes had spoken to a great extent about the power available to Christians in the person of the Holy Spirit.

"Roger," the pastor asked, "do you understand what the Holy Spirit can do in your life? We studied these things soon after we first met."

"No," Roger replied, "I didn't get too much of those things back then, but I am really listening now."

The pastor carefully instructed Roger over an open Bible. He listened avidly, and when he fully understood, Roger opened his heart completely to accept the provision of the Lord Jesus Christ for his victorious living. He saw no lightning, nor did he hear thunder, but his life was changed once more.

At home, Roger tried to tell Shirley what had taken place in his life. He had begun to bubble inside, and longed for her to know the new sense of power and purpose of which he was already aware in his life. She was not slow to grasp the truth of the empowering Holy Spirit, and easily and quickly laid hold on His infilling. A new hunger for God swept over both of their lives, as did an urgency to serve Jesus Christ with all their strength.

Their work together for God became easier as they fully depended upon the power of the Holy Spirit. When Roger wanted to run ahead, as in other days, there was a new restraint to hold him into what God required. While still inexperienced in the ways of the Spirit, Roger nevertheless grew lustily in spiritual and mental faith.

Soon, his testimony came to be known and told in many places. He and Shirley were especially able and competent to help young married people. Their own experience had given them that special touch of understanding which was so much needed.

Part of their empathy with young marrieds sprang from the miracle birth of their son, Joshua. Joshua made his surprising entrance into the world Christmas, 1976. The circumstances surrounding his arrival were such that Roger and Shirley never lost the thrill of sharing the story.

When Roger lay in pain in Great Lakes Naval Hospital, one of the most shattering of his wounds was one which was given to him by the very doctors who were treating him. A surgeon stood at the side of his bed, and with sombre face told Roger, "You will not be able to father any children."

The wounds which Roger suffered in Vietnam had been both visible and invisible. Burning fragments of grenade had entered his groin, and moving upward had done severe damage to the internal organs which controlled the reproductive system. When Roger was finally discharged, he chose to forget this. It would have been ego disturbing to have always had it in mind. Yet, in his marriage, both he and Shirley longed for children of their own. Joshua's arrival became a special miracle.

Shirley had not told Roger she thought she was pregnant. On the excuse of a normal checkup, Shirley went to her doctor. She was right. She was very pregnant. With subtle humor, she sent flowers to Roger at his office, and on the card wrote, "The rabbit died. Love, Shirley." It took the girls at the office to enlighten Roger about the rabbit test. Roger's joy knew no bounds. He wasn't sterile after all!

Over in Okinawa, Roger's twin brother met a man who looked at him in a puzzled way. The navy medic asked Roger's brother if there was another who looked like him. He explained he had been at Great Lakes when a man who was the "spittin' image of you" was a patient. Roger's brother told the man it was his twin brother; he was discharged now, and expecting to be a father any day.

"A father?" the medic questioned in surprise. "There was no way he could ever be a father. I was there when they told him. His prostate was really torn up."

"Well," Roger's brother told him, "they were dead wrong!"

Roger and Shirley were filled with gratitude to God

for the gift of Joshua. When their son was born, their joy was full. At work, on the streets and in the home, life was full. Sometimes Shirley wished Roger could be home more, but the pace of the agency had become so fast as to preclude much time together. Nevertheless, they were happy in what God was doing for them. Shirley called it their honeymoon with Jesus. Possibly, if Roger and Shirley had been able to see ahead a few years, their joy may have been even greater, for God gave them another beautiful child; a little girl, Jamie Leigh, was born in 1981, again attesting to His gentle care for them.

In August 1978, Roger rushed in from an extensive field trip, dressed quickly and went to a study and prayer group. It was a night of destiny for him.

During a time of meditation, the Spirit of God came upon Roger, speaking to him in urgent and insistent words. "Roger, do you love your work more than you love my work?" the voice of God asked.

Roger was thunderstruck. This was the first time he had experienced any challenge concerning his devotion to the cause of Jesus Christ, and his loyalty to the will of God. He felt blown apart with a divine grenade, spiritually shattered with the same severity he had been physically shattered in Vietnam. He was wounded then; he was wounded now.

"God, I believe I love you more than anything in the whole world," he replied.

"Then Roger, would you let your business go, and serve me for the rest of your life?" the Voice asked.

Roger knew he was being asked to surrender everything of this world's interests and fame; literally, he was being asked to die to all the allure and appeal of this world. He felt the pull of the agency, and all the future he and Shirley had planned together. He made an effort to argue the case with God.

"Lord," he returned, "you made me the best in the company. You gave me this job so I could do the things I do. Why would you ask me to leave it all?"

"I have a bigger work for you to do," the Lord responded.

Roger breathed deeply, "Lord, I am willing to serve you, and to do anything you want me to do." Suddenly, a great peace flowed into his heart, and he knew it was indeed the Lord who had communed with him.

As soon as there was an appropriate time, Roger shared with the group what had taken place in his spirit. Someone suggested he was not yet ready for a full-time ministry. He smiled, then replied, "That's God's problem. I'm not asking permission to obey the Lord. I am simply telling you what I intend to do."

Before Roger and Shirley went to bed that night, Roger prayed for stronger faith, and for somebody to confirm what he had determined in his heart. Early next morning, the phone rang. The caller was a man who had not been in the meeting the night before. "Roger," he shared, "last night the Lord told me you must go into full service among the kids on the street."

Roger became unglued. God had both called, and confirmed. Over the days following, other people said the same thing. Roger and Shirley became very sure, very sure.

Next day, Roger wrote his resignation from Pinkerton. He loved the agency in the same passionate way he had loved the Marine Corps. It was a wrenching and tearing thing for him to prepare to leave Pinkerton, alleviated only by the conviction he was doing right. He dated his resignation November 1, 1978.

When the letter was ready, he phoned his immediate chief in Kansas City. "Sir, I would like to come down and talk with you," he said.

The reply was abrupt. "For what?"

"It's personal," he replied. His boss agreed to see him, but left Roger a little perplexed when he said, "I was just getting ready to call you anyway. It can wait until you get here."

The appointment was made for a week ahead. His resignation spelled out the exact reasons for his termination; it expressed his sorrow in leaving and the conviction that God was calling him to work full-time among the beaten kids on the streets. Roger expected to see the regional manager alone, but both the assistant manager and the director of sales were present.

"Well Helle, what can I do for you?" the boss queried.

Roger handed him his resignation. His boss took a long time to digest its contents. Then, he passed it to the other men. When it was fully read, the regional manager looked at Roger, his face registering shock. "Helle," he said, "I've never had such a resignation in all the years I've been with Pinkerton. If you had come down here with any other reason, I'd have tried to argue you out of the resignation.

"Helle, if you were unhappy with anybody on the field, I'd fire him sooner than lose you. If you wanted more money, I'd give you a raise, but I have never had anyone ask me to quit so as to serve God! I wouldn't argue with you if I could. Who can win arguing with God?

"However, I have an obligation to tell you why I had been ready to call you. The executive vice-president of the company has told me you are being considered as assistant director of investigations for the entire nation. You would be on twice your present salary. When the present director retires, you would automatically move into his position. It is the fifth top position in the company, and leads even higher.

"Will you consider this, Helle?"

Roger didn't even find it hard to answer. The call of God was sure and certain. The job offer was attractive, but not enough to change his heart. He knew he could do as well at the offered job as in the present job, but the one God offered was what he wanted to do.

"No sir, but I am honored to be considered," Roger replied.

Later, Roger called his wife and told her of the offer. Shirley wasn't even mildly interested. Roger was greatly encouraged by her commitment to the work to which God had called them. He reminded her of their determination early in the year to excel in business, in order that the world might know who the real winner was in their lives.

"Roger," Shirley said, "we better start planning!"

21
New Battle Plans

Back in Omaha, Roger and Shirley sat down to discuss the future. Neither of them was concerned or worried for what might lie ahead, but both realized the need for a clear path.

The Lighthouse Ministry, which Roger and his wife had now conducted for some years, was a Friday evening to Sunday evening activity. It had a gross budget of $800 each month, and of that sum, a large portion was supplied from the resources they personally possessed. With the resignation from his job, Roger scheduled to finish work on November 10. He knew that with his last pay envelope, part of the money needed for the Lighthouse Ministry would cease. Both he and Shirley found this more disconcerting than anything else. Their hearts were among the kids with whom they worked.

"Shirley," Roger posed, "I brought some good operational guidelines out of Vietnam. When I was leading my men, it was never a haphazard event. I planned each mission and sweep. If I had not done so, I could easily have lost my men.

"Back there, a lot of people thought I loved to kill

and destroy. What they did not know was that had I not been so ruthlessly efficient, it would have been my men and I who would have died. I planned to stay alive, and that demanded that I do my work correctly. I was committed to life, and that involved death for every one of the enemy I could set eyes on.

"Now, we are in the same position. If we do not make every effort to plan, taking into consideration every place where there is danger, we could lose greatly."

Shirley lifted an eyebrow and said nothing. She knew her husband, and figured he was working out a battle plan which would operate for them in the new situation. Roger went on . . .

"I really think we should map out our goals and our objectives. One thing is sure; we know who the enemy is. We must plan to defeat him at every contact. If we don't kill his deployment, he will certainly try to kill what we do."

"But Roger," Shirley objected, "we have no resources for the work. How can we work without the bare necessities?"

"I don't really know yet," Roger countered, "but we do have the power of the Lord working on our side. The Holy Spirit will help us find the way to operate. In the meantime, we have a Christian concert scheduled the same night I bring home my last paycheck. Perhaps the Lord will use something then to show us how to move."

One of the most popular activities of Lighthouse Ministries was the monthly concert for the young people of Omaha. Roger brought many popular Christian musicians to town, and the attendance was always large. On November 10, 1978 he had scheduled such a quality group. When the night came, there was a packed audience. As always, Roger gave a closing invitation for young men and women to give their lives to Jesus Christ. That evening five hundred made the decision to trust Him.

Roger's excitement grew. The response to the work was greater than he had dared imagine. It solved one of the only things which troubled him. His life had been so geared to excitement, both in Vietnam and at Pinkerton, that he wondered whether the more "Christian" activity could satisfy him. Now he really knew!

Serving Christ was more exciting than anything he had ever done. With the help of God, he had rendered five hundred of the enemy's troops powerless, and then converted them over to the side of the Lord. He figured that was a major victory, and all the excitement he could handle. "God, I will never worry about the excitement again. This is all I can support," he vowed in gratitude.

To Shirley he remarked in partial seriousness, "I am glad they made me a professional killer. It was survival then, but now I really do kill the enemy for sheer joy. Imagine darling, five hundred at one time!"

Shirley was as happy as Roger himself. There were many things they did not yet see, but the battle had been joined. In the battle, God had confirmed His will for their lives. Roger had said, "We just want to help people, in whatever way they need help," and the concert had provided the assurance that this was a good and wonderful work.

On the other side of town, a man sat deeply perplexed. For some time now, he had been part of a select committee, appointed to study the feasibility of launching a Teen Challenge Center in Omaha. The outstanding results of David Wilkerson's original work in New York had become a byword across America. Many cities were beginning similar activities, and it was generally believed there should be such a place in Omaha.

Dale had a number of problems. That was nothing new, for in his professional banking career he frequently faced difficulties, if not his own, then someone else's. Still, the problems in the matter before him had resulted in the collapse of the committee. A major difficulty lay in the inability to find committed leaders; and, too, there was the whole problem of funding a center's operation after it was launched.

Then, as though out of nowhere, Roger and Shirley Helle came flying across his frame of knowledge. It was little wonder he was perplexed. They, he felt, were the perfect answer to the stalling of the committee. Dale wasn't sure they would be interested in beginning a Teen Challenge Center, but he knew he had to find out. "After all," he thought, "they can only say no." Comforting himself, he remembered that if the proposal was of God, it would fly against all odds.

In Roger's home, a constant stream of prayer was moving upward. Following the encouragement of the music concert, he and Shirley were involved in trying to lay out a definite plan of battle. They were not getting ahead as quickly as they wished; but then, they didn't know what God was doing on the other side of the city.

Dale picked up his telephone, breathed a prayer and called Roger Helle.

Roger picked up his telephone, breathed a prayer and said, "Roger Helle speaking." A plan established in heaven was under way. A plan which would unfold as time went on, but which, at this early stage was totally unstructured.

"Roger, I would like to invite you to meet a committee this Monday evening. We would like to talk with you about your work, and about what we are interested in doing in Omaha. Could you and your wife meet us on Monday night?" Dale did not elaborate, but Roger, always seeking the mind of the Lord in his situation, gladly agreed to the meeting.

Perhaps Dale's committee thought Roger should know about Teen Challenge. After all, didn't everybody? Wasn't the name of David Wilkerson common on the lips of every Christian? In any case, Dale and his committee said little to Roger about the work of Teen Challenge, but rather showed a great interest in the work of Lighthouse Ministry.

Roger shared all he could, but time after time he came back to a basic premise which he and Shirley had adopted, "We just want to help people in whatever way they are hurting." He and his wife were in that best of all times, when they had an emerging theology, no hang-ups and oceans of yearning for people. It represented a winning combination to Dale and his committee. The group prayed together, and Roger and Shirley went home to continue to pray by themselves.

Dale picked up his phone again. The committee was fully convinced Roger and Shirley were the people they were looking for. "Can you meet with us again on Friday evening?" he asked Roger.

On that Friday evening, history was written into the life of Omaha, Nebraska. Roger said, "Yes," and the committee said, "Praise the Lord!"

With the work of the committee finished, there was

no more for them to do except to pray God's blessing upon these two who would carry the flag of Christian witness into the depths of the drug culture. They gave nothing to Roger and Shirley except their encouragement, and the right to use the name of Teen Challenge.

"Shirley," Roger enthused, "we are away and running again. At least we know what we have to do now. We must commence by finding out what others do in the same situation."

In Denver, Kansas City and even in New York, Roger and Shirley watched the existing centers at work. Not everything he saw pleased Roger. It became very apparent to him, that operations which might succeed in one city, would not necessarily be of value in another. "It's just like 'Nam again," he told Shirley. "Just like Pinkerton, too. We found we had to use originality in Pinkerton; we will have to do the same here." Roger and Shirley evaluated more than a dozen centers.

There was not a great deal they could do on the very slender resources left to them. When they had finished the round of orientation visits, Roger and Shirley sat down to develop a policy and philosophy for Omaha.

"Let's write down what it is we feel, honey," he said to Shirley. They sat down and made a list of the things they thought were imperative for them.

"First, we will never run co-ed houses," Roger began. "It is a major hindrance to achievement. Most of the people we will work with come out of depravity, sex and drugs. We need to give them encouragement to win with Christ, rather than putting them back where they come under strain." Shirley totally agreed.

As they formed the philosophy of operation, they

made a solemn determination for the future. They would never make decisions unilaterally; they would always agree together. Otherwise they would shelve the proposal.

"And Roger, we must major on smooth staff relationships, the same way you operated with your men, and with the staff at Pinkerton," Shirley offered.

"That's for sure," Roger replied. "There must be team operation. There isn't any room for a bird colonel with all the rest buck privates. That's a good way to get let down in a pinch. The staff will have many good ideas, and we want to give them the OK to think for themselves.

"I will also need," Roger added, "to be very careful to delegate authority and to trust those I assign to work. Men and women respond best when trusted. The fact is, I can't afford to be threatened. I need to get the best, and be the best. For sure, we don't have all the answers."

During their traveling, Roger and Shirley found there were varying degrees of interest in outreach evangelism. They recognized it would be easy to see the center as the main, even only responsibility. Roger's burden for people was so great it required more than the work with the inmates of a drug rehabilitation house.

"Let's plan big for soul-winning, Shirley," he suggested.

"What do you think we ought to do?" she asked.

Roger replied that he felt they should continue the success of the concerts, and then plan to do up to six full-scale summer outreach crusades in neighboring towns and cities. "You see, honey, the more we put out, the more God will allow us to take in. I saw the outreach idea in New York, and I think we can reach a doper on a street corner, when we can't get him to enter the formal house program. We can major the distribution of tracts, Bibles and other Christian literature. The outreach must be on a saturation basis, and use as much volunteer help as friendly churches will provide."

With the battle plans ready, Roger and Shirley began to take stock of how they could raise the support needed to do the work. Whimsically, Shirley remarked, "You would think we would be deluged with everything we needed. Everyone who has read about Teen Challenge gets all misty-eyed. I heard of one man who was reading *The Cross and the Switchblade* while he was driving down the freeway in Los Angeles. His emotion got so great he pulled off the Santa Ana Freeway onto the shoulder and cried. A California Highway patrolman stopped behind him to discover what was wrong. When the man told him the truth, the patrolman said, 'I should write you a citation, but you see, I have just read the book, too.'"

With great care, Roger and Shirley began to form a list of friends and fellow-Christians they knew. It grew very slowly, but as time went on, the support began to dribble in. Soon there was a marginal support base, and the work was taking shape.

Roger was grateful to God for the permanent pension which was a result of the wounds he had suffered in Vietnam. There was never an excess in their home and kitchen, but there was always something.

The hand of the Lord had set the battle lines, and the warriors were ready. Roger was in his Christian service, the same as in an earth battle. He allowed no

room for retreat, no quarter to the enemy and no toler-
ance to cowardice. He and Shirley made their solemn
commitment on their knees, praying, "Lord, you have
given us this battle to win. In the power and strength of
your spirit we will take the battle to the enemy, striking
him with everything you have, and everything we
have."

Down in hell, the devil heard and trembled.

22
Early Successes

It took the first six months to complete the plans for the work of Teen Challenge. When Roger felt the future had some shape to it, he began to look for a place where he could establish the headquarters of the work. Property prices were grossly inflated, and he began to despair of finding suitable premises. He looked over many older and large houses, but was not able to put together a deal he was happy with. When he exhausted every avenue he knew, there was little else to do but pray. Roger and Shirley prayed.

During the waiting time, opportunities began to come for Roger to tell others of the plans for Teen Challenge. Many churches in Nebraska heard of the plans to establish a center. From these early opportunities the support base began to enlarge. People grew excited as they heard of the scope of the vision. Roger was determined to develop a program for those who would not be able to come into the house program. He called it his "Out-patient Program."

From where he stood, it appeared that nothing was available for younger teenagers. What help was there for a recalcitrant fifteen-year-old teenager? Roger saw that nothing was being done in the area of counseling service for people of this age group. His main concern was to establish the center, but while that was pending, there were other things which needed to be done. These he developed as far as he could.

Toward the end of the first quarter of 1979, Roger was contacted by a leading realtor in Omaha who knew of the search for property.

"I want you to come and see a house," he said.

Roger had seen dozens of properties so the opportunity to see one more was not especially exciting. He agreed to see the house however, and as he prepared to meet the man, Roger reflected upon an interesting situation in his search. It seemed to him that each likely place he saw became a little bigger. Initially, he had looked at houses which had two thousand square feet; then it was three thousand. One day he said to Shirley, "You know, I keep getting the feeling that when the Lord takes us to the place He has in mind, it will be a mansion. Perhaps He knows we will eventually need more room." These thoughts were in his mind when he left to meet the realtor. The man had said it was a "big old mansion."

As Roger sat with the realtor, he was amazed to learn that the house was immediately opposite the existing coffee shop where he had worked with kids for some years. The building was owned by Planned Parenthood. He wondered how he had not had the place registered in his mind before. He knew he must have looked over that way every time he was at the coffee shop.

The realtor pulled his car up in front of the building,

and Roger whistled. A massive old home mastered his vision. "How big is that place?" he asked, with emphasis on the verb.

"Sixty-four hundred square feet, and a hundred years waiting here for you," the realtor answered.

Roger walked, a little breathlessly, toward the house. The Lord broke into his thoughts, speaking clearly to his spirit, "This is your house. I am going to give it to you for seventy-five thousand dollars."

The building was on the market at one hundred and ten thousand dollars. The price had come down to a bedrock of ninety-five thousand; The Lord was saying seventy-five! Roger reached for his faith and tucked the information away in his heart. He could not see how the lower price was to eventuate.

"Let's begin to pray about the house and the price," he suggested to Shirley. Wherever he spoke he lined up the prayer battalions. Heaven was battered with the intensity of the stream of prayer and intercession.

From August until January the prayer vigil went on. At the same time, Roger continued negotiations with the realtor. There was no way that Planned Parenthood was willing to bend in the matter of the price, but God has said seventy-five thousand dollars, and Roger was not willing to budge either.

Then the Lord stepped in to use His secret weapon!

When the original listing was made, the commitment was given by the realtor to purchase the house himself at seventy-five thousand dollars. Only God and the parties knew of that commitment. It was to become operative if the house did not sell by the date of the listing period. That time had come.

"Roger," the realtor said, "how important is it to

you to get that property?"

"Hey man," Roger replied, "God said that was my house. That was all I needed. If I heard God right, then I need it in the worst way."

"I hear you," the man said.

Roger had not told anyone except Shirley about the word of the Lord concerning the price. The realtor did not know; the members of Roger's own board did not know; nobody knew. Everyone knew Roger felt it was God's answer to the need, but more than that Roger had not communicated.

Down at the bank where Dale worked, the realtor chatted with him. During the conversation, Dale felt an urgent need to give the realtor a copy of *The Cross and the Switchblade*, with an explanation about the work of Teen Challenge, and the in-birth status of the Omaha center.

The realtor read the book with profound emotion. It moved him deeply. The long expected profit on a certain huge old house no longer seemed important. "I can sell it to them at the price I said I would give to the listing party," he reflected. He had never mentioned such a figure to Roger.

Next day the realtor phoned Dale. "Listen, I can get that place for seventy-five thousand dollars. Do you think your man would be interested?"

"I'll talk to him," Dale replied. Then he phoned Roger with excitement. "I have inside information about that house, Roger. I have reason to believe you can get it for seventy-five thousand dollars."

Roger laughed over that phone line. "Dale, I have had inside information that I can buy that house for seventy-five thousand dollars for almost six months!"

On January 11, 1980, the "big old mansion" became the headquarters of Teen Challenge of the Midlands. When national interest rates were almost out of sight, the realtor sold it to Roger for the sum God had stipulated and at ten and one-half percent interest!

As the news of the acquisition became known, people came to help with the restoration. Three men walked in off the street one day, each looking tough and mean. Roger tensed as they came toward him, thinking they were not meaning any good. "What is this place?" one of them grunted. Roger explained the plans for the center.

"We heard this was to be a Teen Challenge place," another of the men said. "We are all electricians, and right now we have nothing to do. We would like to offer to do any work you need done in our field." Dumbfounded, but very grateful, Roger put the men to work. They did other things in addition to the needed electrical work. They hung plasterboard, stripped walls and made themselves almost indispensable.

With assistance from many people, the work on the "big old mansion" moved right along. Roger and Shirley gave July 6 to their board as a probable opening date.

In June of 1980, Roger received an invitation to speak about Teen Challenge in Des Moines, Iowa. During his visit, he was motoring with the pastor. The man said, "You know, Roger, we have a real need for a similar program here in Iowa. What you are doing in Omaha needs to be done here. Some time ago, a man offered me the use of a very large, old fraternity house if I wanted to start something. My board turned it down."

As they drove on, they chatted about the old house and its virtues. Roger began to tingle all over. Later, he described the feeling as similar to the one he felt when there was action about to break leading his patrols in Vietnam. The hair stood up on the back of his neck, and he became very aware of spiritual action about to break.

On the way back from the meeting, Roger asked his friend to show him the house. He just had to see it, although the idea of developing anything in Des Moines seemed absurd. He was still believing God for the completion of the Omaha house, for carpet, for the down payments on utilities and a host of other, less expensive items. Poised, and only a month from the scheduled date of opening in Omaha, Roger thought he already had plenty to do. The man agreed to show him the house, however, if just to satisfy Roger's curiosity.

Once again Roger experienced a sizing shock. The house was not just any ordinary place. Even though it was broken down, dilapidated and dirty, its potential shone through. The house had more than ten thousand square feet of floor space. It seemed huge to Roger, and his mind began to do somersaults as he saw its possibilities. The owner came over and made Roger an offer to rent it to him for seven hundred dollars a month.

"For ten thousand square feet?!" Roger thought.

Roger's board was made up of conservative Christian businessmen. He wondered how they would react to the idea of trying to open two houses instead of one. He figured it might have been better had Omaha already been open, but nevertheless he determined to launch out in faith with God. The rental was little more than the principal and interest payments on the Omaha property.

The consummation of the deal required twenty-two hundred dollars. By the time it had reached that stage, Roger was present at a church conference in Des Moines. After one of the sessions, a couple came to Roger with some embarrassment. "You might think this is weird," the man said, "but today the Lord told us to give you this check for one thousand dollars. He said you would need it."

After the evening session, a youth pastor took Roger and Shirley out for refreshments. While they were eating, an identical thing took place. "Roger," the man said, "the Lord told us to give you this check for twelve hundred dollars. We do not understand why, but you will know."

With the security deposits in hand and the utility deposits guaranteed, Roger signed the papers to rent the house in Des Moines for a year.

The Omaha center was scheduled to open as a center for men. In the reshuffling, Omaha became the house for women, and Des Moines, the center for men. Des Moines opened on the first anniversary of Roger's severance from Pinkerton Detective Agency. He recognized the goodness of God.

Although there were some misgivings among his board members as to the wisdom of being spread so thin, Roger was deeply grateful to them for their continued support. The work of Teen Challenge was now fully launched. Both houses had students in their programs, and the full potential of the work was now clear. Roger and Shirley were no longer a team of two. They had retained staff for both houses, and the process of screening applications for admission to the rehabilitation program was refined.

With the work load double that which had been originally considered, Roger and his wife became very busy. From side to side of Nebraska and across Iowa, they took the message of their ministry. Human derelicts were being salvaged by the power of the gospel of Jesus Christ; their lives were opened to the surging power of the Holy Spirit and the fellowship of Christians.

"Shirley," Roger commented, "I am certainly glad we took the time to establish our goals and working philosophies. The work is now leading us instead of we leading it."

23
Taking Casualties

With both centers full and flying, Roger hoped he could concentrate upon the actual responsibilities of the work. Certainly, he never dreamed of the enormity of some of the things which would happen in the day-by-day operation of the centers. Perhaps, he might even have lost a clear vision of the real identity of the enemy; he was so totally engrossed with the lives of the students, the applications for entry and the need to continually seek support to maintain the levels of ministry.

During the first six months of the Omaha house, the students accepted had all been women. The switch to Des Moines had not yet taken place, and the work was not yet catering to the needs of men. Somewhere near the middle of 1980, Roger was out of town on a speaking engagement; the enemy took the opportunity to spring the first major problem.

One of Roger's assistants became alerted to a strange relationship which had developed between two of the women students. He was so burdened about the situation he called Roger with his concern, "Roger, I really believe there is something wrong with the relationship between those two gals."

Roger found it very hard to accept. One was a supervisor, the other a counselor. He did remember, however, that when the supervisor requested permission to particularly disciple the other girl, he had been restrained in his spirit. Only after much insistence had he yielded to the request. The permission was, apparently, back to haunt him.

Back in Des Moines, he faced the situation head-on, understanding again the power of the enemy to disrupt. He called Betty into conference, confronting her with the allegation of her homosexual relationship with Pam.

"Betty," he opened, "it is commonly believed you are involved in an improper relationship with Pam. For some time there has been a change in your disposition to me and to the work. I have not wanted to believe it was caused by anything more than the strain of the work, but numbers of the girls have observed there is more than that to this thing. I want you to be honest with me. Is this charge true?"

Roger was to face then a fact of Christian work. He discovered the bitterness which eats away at one who is living in sin. Betty erupted into a violent denunciation of him, and a rabid defense of her right to sexual freedom.

In the days when he and Shirley mapped out the philosophy of the work, they had determined that in all cases where an actual discipline was required, it would be administered in a spirit of love and tenderness. Roger knew that the whole purpose of biblical discipline was ultimate restoration. He now found out it was simpler to deal with someone already repentant than with someone who was stubborn and unrepentant.

Betty and Pam were discharged from the program. It was the first crushing blow since the opening of the work. Roger and Shirley were devastated, but they did as they knew they must do. Lovingly, but firmly, they reasoned with the girls before sending them away.

"Shirley," Roger asked, "what do you think will happen to those girls? They are grown women, and both have made real efforts to live for God. Surely the enemy will not take them out altogether."

Shirley looked at him with compassion. She knew how much this disturbance had hurt him, and she knew he needed assurance which only she could give. "Roger, you have done what the Lord expected of you. You sent them away with love, and you told them you would pray for the day when they would put the thing right. I believe you can rest your case. Someday Betty and Pam will put it right with God, and with you. It was very important that you took the stand you did. Now all the students know that sin will not be tolerated if it is known. We must take this position, Roger. It is the only way we can build a permanent and stable work."

Roger was comforted. He followed the relationship with his prayers, and when the girls were long separated from each other, both came independently to Roger to ask for his forgiveness, and to try to pick up the threads of active Christian life again.

Shirley had been most supportive, but she had a special burden to bear. Day by day, Shirley was the oversight authority in the center. Matters of staff were her responsibility and concern. She plainly felt she had failed. It was one thing to know that right had been done, but another to put it all behind. She grieved over the loss of a trusted worker, one in whom she had placed great confidence. In some kind of psychological depression, she struggled slowly to cope with this reverse. Finally, she came to know that both Roger and she had to let the thing go, and leave the ultimate dispositions with the Lord. The family had been bereaved, but in the sorrow there were others being born into it regularly. The work had taken a casualty of large proportion, but the mainstream of the work must go on.

From time to time, others dropped out of the program. Since there was no way to evaluate the probabilities of success when a person applied for entry, Roger and Shirley came to see there would be a percentage of loss. Knowing the inevitability of this, the two worked very hard to create a sense of "family" in the centers. Their disappointment was always acute when another casualty occurred, but they soon discovered that such events called for immediate regrouping, evaluation and assessment. As time went on, they became more sensitive to the signs and symptoms which were always given by those in danger of collapse, and were able to contain the threat in many cases.

Unfortunately, not all the casualties were among those who had come through the program. They were hard to take, but at least the loss was understandable. There were sad defections among others.

From the deep south came a woman to work as a secretary, highly recommended by a leading personality. Roger was induced to trust her with much responsibility. After a period of time, it became clear that monies were disappearing from a number of sources; large gasoline bills were charged against the center. Finally, when the woman tried to place a donated car into her own name, the facts began to pour out.

"Why have you done this?" Roger confronted the woman.

Once again he was faced with an unrepentant heart. She acted as though it were her right to use the money and resources of the Lord. It was a sad farewell, as well as a long trip back to her home state.

Casualties!

Nothing in all of these things was able to divert the hearts of Roger and Shirley from the task to which they had given their hands. The call of God was becoming almost obsessive in their lives. This was the work to which they were assigned. Their orders had been cut in the orderly room of heaven, and carried the signature of the Lord Jesus Christ, written in His blood. They sought no relief from the burden and challenge.

Then came the fire. Neither wind nor storm had affected them in any permanent sense. But the fire . . . that was different.

In August 1984, the enemy mounted a counterattack which seemed to bring the work to a standstill. By this time, the work of Teen Challenge had spread considerably. In addition to the two main centers in Omaha and Des Moines, the work now included two other centers. While not fully operational as the larger works, these two centers provided emergency help to local churches whose pastors were puzzled with the problems of case disposition. The work had never seemed stronger. Some months earlier, Roger and Shirley had gone through a time of intense exercise with God as to what their vision for the future really involved. They felt they knew where God wanted them to take the work in the future, and they were all set to implement the expansions which were in their hearts.

Roger was in Davenport leading a team of workers on one of the summer outreach efforts. Early in the morning on August 8, the Holy Spirit awakened him to pray. As he prayed, a quiet, insistent message came to him, "Go home to Omaha." As he considered the message, he was aware of no great foreboding, only the need to obey. He called his workers together and explained that he needed to return home, and then left them to finish the crusade.

In Omaha Roger found everything normal. He spent the day of August 9 resting and studying in the Word of God. He could see no immediate reason for his return, but he did not have long to wait for the clarification of the directive.

At 5:45 A.M. on August 10, the phone jangled beside his head. He reached for it to hear the wife of one of his staff members say, "Roger, there has been a fire at Teen Challenge. Everything is OK, I think." The woman sounded very calm, and assured Roger that everyone was safely out of the house. Promising her he would be there shortly, he dressed and left for the Center.

As he topped a hill above the area where the house was located, he could see flames bursting from the structure. A huge pall of smoke hung over the neighborhood. A terrible sinking feeling developed in him.

"God, O God—please no!" he cried.

All the work of the years was going up in flames. In that house was the investment of his life, both in people and in physical assets. He saw firemen on the roof, fire trucks all around the house and a crowd of people watching.

Roger drove into the area, shocked to see an ambulance in the driveway. Screaming tires brought him to a stop. There in front of him were the girls from the house. Roger dashed up to Steve, the husband of the woman who had called him, and asked, "What's happened Steve?"

Steve was standing mute with tears running down his face. In an effort to pull himself together, he looked at Roger and said, "Sandy is dead."

Roger felt as though he had been hit with a grenade again. He felt himself spinning and falling. It was the reenactment of an earlier nightmare. The real significance was not yet dawning on him. As with all explosions, the pain waits, so the pain was slow in coming. "What?" he said. "What did you say, Steve?"

"Sandy is dead," Steve repeated.

Sandy dead? At twenty-seven years of age, everyone loved Sandy. She couldn't be dead. Roger looked over toward the drive and caught sight of a body under a sheet. With an appalling understanding of hundreds of similar sights in Vietnam, the truth broke in upon Roger. The burning house, the body of a loved student, the weeping girls, the ambulance and the fire trucks, all combined to break him. His vision before God was all gone, he realized; then he broke into tears. Nobody had ever seen Roger cry. They looked at him sympathetically as he wandered among the chaos.

Roger jolted. A voice was speaking to him, but there was nobody beside him. It was jeering, contemptible and laughing, "You will never, not ever do anything for the Kingdom of God again!" He stood weeping while the enemy taunted and abused him. It was the lowest time in Roger's life.

The fire chief approached Roger. "Are you the

Director?" he asked. When receiving assurance he added, "We think the gas stove exploded in the kitchen, and the girl was unable to get out."

Roger asked him how badly Sandy was burned. He was again shocked to be told she was burned beyond recognition. "Sandy, Sandy," he murmured to himself. "Thank God you had accepted Jesus into your life."

Slowly, self-control returned to Roger. He realized there were many things urgently requiring his attention, things no one else was able to do. As after so many horrendous battle scenes in Vietnam, Roger knew a massive regrouping would be needed. His mind and heart were scarred with the flames which had taken Sandy's life. He felt he would never be the same again; this was a wound from which recovery would be slow.

The Omaha newspapers gave extensive coverage to the story. Suddenly it seemed the whole purpose of Teen Challenge was exposed to the world. People talked about the horror of drug abuse, and the efforts of Teen Challenge to bring the reality of Jesus Christ to those whose lives had been so terribly hurt in the subculture of the drug scene. In a very special sense, it seemed Sandy may have achieved more in her death than in her life.

Roger received an outpouring of comfort, sympathy and prayer from across the nation. Leading clergymen and local politicians sent their condolences and encouragement.

In the quietness of their home and in the security of Shirley's love, Roger let his grief be controlled by the ministration of the Holy Spirit. His wife knew it would be just fine after Roger said to her one day, "With God's help, we will rise again."

24
God Wins

The enemy had made a significant counterattack. In the ferocity of the fire, Roger had no choice but to pull back and estimate the losses.

The death of Sandy brought a cloud of sorrow over the entire work. The girls in the program at Omaha required to be accommodated and protected from greater injury. The work on the Des Moines house was progressing, but was not yet completed. In every sector of the work, there were many things which needed careful consideration.

Roger and Shirley were brought into an even closer bond in the service of the Lord Jesus. They recognized it would need all their best efforts in God to overcome the many problems which were the natural result of the tragedy. Roger was unable to forget the mocking and cruel words of the Devil, and he was determined the adversary would not make them come true.

In the eye of the storm, not once did Roger ask God why this had happened. He never questioned the omniscience of the Lord. Rather, he began immediately to think in terms of starting the work again. The fire, he figured, was the work of the enemy, whose job it was to "kill and destroy" the interests of the Lord Jesus.

Nevertheless, Roger knew he needed to hear from God in the distress and perplexities of the time. He prayed with great earnestness, "I need to hear from you, God, to know what you want me to do now." In actuality, he had cried out this way while still weeping at the fire. Shirley had arrived, and Roger held her in his arms as the flames roared. Right there he asked for direction, and the Lord intervened even then to speak to his heart.

Down the road, eight blocks from Teen Challenge, lived a couple who had been close friends of the Helle's for years. At the time of the fire, the man was leaving his home to take his wife to work. The radio announcer made the suggestion that people needing to go in the vicinity of 58th and Maple take alternate routes due to a fire in the Benson Shopping area. Bill looked at his wife and said, "That fire is in Teen Challenge. Let's go!" There was no way he could have known the location of the fire, apart from direct illumination of the Holy Spirit.

As they hurried toward the fire, Bill heard the Lord tell him to take a message to Roger. "Give him Isaiah 41:10," the Lord directed. Bill didn't know what it said, and had no Bible with him to check the passage. He and his wife pulled in to the location of the fire, and as they came to a stop, saw Roger holding Shirley; both of them were weeping. Bill and his wife rushed to their friends, putting protecting arms around them. Bill delivered the message at just the time Roger was calling out to God for knowledge and guidance.

Roger walked to his car and took out his modern version of the Scriptures. He turned to the passage and read, "Do not fear, for I am with you; Do not anxiously look about you, for I am your God. I will strengthen you, surely I will help you, Surely I will uphold you with My righteous right hand" (*NASB*).

The message was incredibly powerful to Roger. The fire was raging; the firemen were breaking windows and ripping out boards to try to get to the seat of the blaze.

God said, "Do not anxiously look about you!" From that moment, Roger knew that in some way, God would ultimately be glorified in the events of that morning.

Beginning the day after the fire, the enemy rushed other attacks on the reeling Teen Challenge Center.

The damage to the property was more than one hundred thousand dollars and to the contents, twenty-five thousand dollars. Roger looked in dismay at the fire insurance policy. It was for seventy-seven thousand dollars, and related to the structure only.

The gaunt skeleton of the house was boarded up; the staff did not wish to enter the place again, and everything seemed to indicate the center would never be reopened. Some of Roger's board members felt the place should not reopen, and the City of Omaha vetoed the whole project. The city discovered the zoning was incorrect for such work, and the Health Department said they required a special permit based on proper zoning before they would allow the use of the building.

With all the bureaucratic red tape, Roger felt totally powerless. His dismay grew as a Christian contractor estimated that, even with every corner being cut, the physical damage was far in excess of a full insurance settlement.

Then, the axe fell one more time. The insurance

company found an excuse to lift the value of the property and thereby penalize the policy. They were willing to pay fifteen thousand dollars less than the face amount.

Roger looked at the adjustment manager and said, "There is no way we can rebuild if you do this. Let me tell you something. That is God's money you are playing with. If you are going to do this, there is someone I can talk to about it." Roger meant he could talk with the Lord; the insurance company thought he was threatening legal action! Roger won, and the company paid out the full face value of the policy. It was a turning in the way. The picture was that much less bleak.

The City Zoning Department which had adamantly refused to grant a permit for the reconstruction, continued to obstruct all progress. "God," Roger prayed, "they say there is no way they can alter their position. They refuse to make an exception."

The Lord spoke to Roger. "Roger, I will make a way where there is no way." The Zoning Commission met, and Roger scarcely had time to rise and introduce himself.

A lady stood to speak. "We of the zoning commission have looked at this case from every angle. While the application for an exemption is not within the letter of the law, it is within the spirit of the law. We have decided to grant the application for the exemption."

Dazed, but very happy, Roger left the chambers.

With two barriers down, Roger faced the next in line. The City Council had demanded a special Group Care Permit, requiring an appearance before the Council.

Once again, Roger trembled. His name was called, and after normal preliminaries, the president of the City Council addressed the Council.

"We have here," he said, "an application from one of the finest organizations in America." At some length, he spoke of the worth of Teen Challenge, and of the work it had done in the cities of the nation. He recommended the permit be granted forthwith. The Council agreed; and once again, Roger, those who were present to speak favorably and his attorney, were not asked to speak a word. Three barriers were down.

Finally, the reconstruction began. The staff, along with many volunteers, did over thirty thousand dollars worth of work. A Christian businessman donated twenty thousand dollars worth of aluminum siding, and the entire exterior was covered artistically. The problem of total painting was solved.

From November 1984 until March 1985 the work went on. In every area of construction, the results were far better than the original. New carpet was installed throughout, and a totally new kitchen facility was placed in position.

A friend had said to Roger at the time of the fire, "The Lord would remind you of His word in Haggai 2:8-9, 'The silver is Mine, and the gold is Mine,' declares the Lord of hosts. 'The latter glory of this house will be greater than the former'" (*NASB*).

So it came to pass, that the Word of the Lord might be fulfilled. In May 1985, the house opened again in splendor and glory. In no way did it seem like the old building. It was nicer and much more beautiful than the previous structure.

Roger and Shirley bowed again before the Lord, making a new commitment to Him and to the work. "God," Roger affirmed, "we yield ourselves totally to you, to do your will and your work. Let your glory fill us and your power enable us. We dedicate the new house to you, and ourselves with it."

"Roger, it is a serious thing to make promises to the Lord," Shirley remarked one day. "We need to be sure to keep our word to God, lest the power of His Spirit be withdrawn from us."

Roger looked appreciatively at his wife. How mature she has become, he reflected. He could see the compassion and love of Christ in her eyes. He agreed with her, being glad for the way in which the Lord had reminded him to be stable and consistent. Roger grew quiet as he thought. Shirley looked at him, and asked, "What's going on in your head? You have that very special look. Share with me, please."

"Darling, I don't quite know where to begin," Roger replied. "My mind has been flying over the years—all the way back to Vietnam. I recognize how completely the Lord protected me, even when I was wounded. I thought I was tough in those days, but really it was God's providence preparing me for the future. Then, Pinkerton. They were great years, because in them we came to know peace with God, and real love for one another."

Roger paused, as though to be sure he knew what he wanted to say to Shirley, then continued, "Do you remember when I was all bothered about whether there would be enough excitement in the work of God to satisfy that part of me that was always looking for adventure?" Shirley nodded; he carried right on speaking.

"I thought the night when five hundred kids accepted Christ was the answer, and I guess it was. Now I see that there has been nothing but excitement ever since. Who would possibly imagine that God would allow as much to come into our lives as He has. I mean, you and I have seen it all. I heard a man speak recently about the continuing presence of the Lord. He said, 'We all come to times when we look at where we have been and say, "Hitherto hath the Lord helped us,"' [1 Sam. 7:12, *KJV*] and that is just about what I feel in these days. God has been with us as we served Him, and promises to stay with us to the end."

Finally, Roger seemed to run out of words. Shirley had wisely heard him out, and now she had something to say. It was the summing up of all the past and the confidence of all the future.

"Roger darling," she began, "it seems that life is made up of battles. We have just come through a very major struggle. We suffered casualties and were wounded as we fought. One thing seems to stand out in it all . . . "

Tears welled up in her eyes and in the next fleeting moments she looked at the man whose life she shared. She knew his strength, resolve and determination. She knew he still did not have the concept of defeat in his vocabulary, and that already his vision was years ahead; she knew he gloried in the fact the enemy had not beaten them in the struggle.

She paused to look down through the coming years at the river of men and women who would live again as a result of Roger's commitment to Christ. She saw them passing by, each with a special joy in the forgiving mercy of Jesus Christ.

A beautiful smile lit the face of Shirley Metzger Helle. Through her tears she looked into Roger's face, and quietly affirmed, " . . . God wins."

Postscript

It has been a long way from Toledo, Ohio. My years in the Marine Corps are becoming only a memory. Too proud then, but willing now for the job for which my life had been spared, Shirley and I have discovered the rewards of obedience.

I was a man whose body had been shattered by a terrible war. The doctors had told me I would never be able to have children. I had given up thinking about it and accepted it as a permanent condition.

We longed for a child, and the Lord, my new Commander—the One who had heard my first prayer in Vietnam when I prayed to live—heard my prayer again. I now asked Him, "Let my wife conceive and bear my child."

I could never cease to follow this Commander, if for no other reason than that Joshua Paul Helle and Jamie Leigh Helle walk, run, and laugh around our home as constant reminders that another prayer for life has been answered.

Today there is a real sense in which I am dead. The past is gone. It's a new life, one filled with excitement, great privilege, and responsibility, sharing my life with those in the gutters, sharing my faith with those who have none of their own.

—Roger Helle